First Dictionary

DP

DEMPSEY
PARR

How to use your dictionary

First Dictionary is a book that tells you about words. It tells you how to spell words and it tells you what words mean. It also shows you how to use words. It has been specially written for people who are just starting to learn to read and write. Most of the words are the kind that you see and use every day and we have given examples of how to use them in simple, easy-to-understand language.

To make the best use of your dictionary, you need to understand how it works. Here are some of its key features.

Alphabetical order

All the words are in the order of the **ABC** - so all words beginning with **A** are grouped together and come before the group of words beginning with **B**; and these **B** words come before words beginning with **C**... and so on all the way to **Z**. The coloured letters on the opposite page shows you the order of the alphabet.

Same but different

You will also discover that there are some words with different meanings but exactly the same spelling.

Carefully selected entries

There are more than 1,500 specially selected entries, or headwords. These are printed in **bold** type.

For example, if you want to find out more about the word **different**, first of all you go to that part of the book where all the words starting with the letter **d** begin. Then you start looking for words beginning with **di**, and then words beginning with **dif**, and so on until you find the word.

bat

1 A **bat** is an animal that looks like a mouse with wings. **Bats** hunt for food at night.

2 A **bat** is also a kind of wooden or metal stick. You use a **bat** for hitting the ball in games such as baseball or cricket.

Clear definitions

Next to the word is the definition. The definition is the part which tells us what the word means. This is written clearly and simply.
So if you look up the definition of **different** you find that it means "not the same".

different
Different means not the same.
These houses are different in twelve ways. Can you see how?

Example sentences

These show you how to use many of the words. They are written in *italic* text.

Helpful illustrations

Every page has carefully chosen illustrations and photographs that help to make the meaning of a word even clearer.

First
Dictionary

Author
John Grisewood

Editor
Angela Crawley

Designer
Rachael Stone

Project Management
Raje Airey

Artwork Commissioning
Susanne Bull

Photography
Patrick Spillane

Photographic Co-ordinator
Lesley Bermingham

Editorial Assistant
Jenni Cozens

Additional editorial help from
Ian Paulyn and Sean Connolly

Editorial Director
Paula Borton

First published in 1998 by
Dempsey Parr
13 Whiteladies Road
Clifton
Bristol
BS8 1PB

Produced by Miles Kelly Publishing Ltd
The Bardfield Centre, Great Bardfield, Essex CM7 4SL

British Library Cataloguing-in-Publication Data
A catalogue record for this book is available from the British Library

ISBN 1 84084 056 0

Printed in Spain

abcdefghijklmnopqrstuvwxyz

octopus *(octopuses)*
An **octopus** is a sea animal with a soft round body and eight long arms called tentacles. **Octopuses** live at the bottom of the sea. They hide in caves and eat crabs and shellfish.

sew *(sews sewing sewed sewn)*
When you **sew**, you use a needle and thread to join pieces of cloth together, or to fix things to cloth. *Zoe is sewing a button on her shirt.*

Finding out about words
When looking up words in this dictionary you will discover that most words have different forms. These are shown after the **headword** and are in *italic* type.

The *plural* form is when there is more than one of something. We make a simple plural by adding an "s" or "es" to the end of certain words *(nouns)*.

The plural form of **octopus** is **octopuses**.

If you add different endings to other kinds of words *(verbs)* you can show when something is happening or has happened.

This tells us that Zoe is sewing the button on her shirt now.

By making these kinds of discoveries you will learn something about how to use words correctly. This is called *grammar*.

Extra everyday words
Last of all, at the end of your dictionary there are some useful facts and a list of words that we use all the time. We all know what these words mean but sometimes may not know how to spell them.

We hope you will enjoy using your First Dictionary and exploring the world of words and their meanings. We also hope you will find it a useful reference book for many years to come as you find out more and more about how language works.

Aa

abroad
If you go **abroad**, you go to another country. *We went abroad for our holidays last year.*

accident
An **accident** is something bad that you did not expect to happen. *I had an accident with the pot of paint. I dropped it and it spilled everywhere.*

ache
An **ache** is a pain in a part of your body that goes on hurting for a long time. *Sam is going to the dentist because he has toothache.*

acrobat
An **acrobat** is a person who can do difficult and exciting balancing tricks. *We watched the acrobats walking along a wire high above the ground.*

act *(acts acting acted)*
If you **act** in a film or play, you play a part in it.

active
Somebody who is **active** moves about a lot and is always very busy doing things.

actor
An **actor** is a person who pretends to be somebody else in a film or play. *That film we saw on TV had really good actors in it.*

add *(adds adding added)*
1 When you **add** something, you put it with something else. *Elliott added sugar to the cake mixture.*
2 When you **add** numbers, you put them together. *If you add three and six you get nine.*

address *(addresses)*
Your **address** is the name of the house, street and town where you live. *Dan's address is 24 River Road, Oaktown OK1 2AD.*

adult
An **adult** is a grown-up person.

adventure
An **adventure** is something exciting or dangerous that happens to you. *Ali's first trip in an aeroplane was quite an adventure.*

advertisement
An **advertisement** in a newspaper or on television tells you about something and tries to make you want to buy it. **Advertisements** are also known as adverts or ads.

aeroplane
An **aeroplane** is a machine that flies. **Aeroplanes** have wings and one or more engines.

afford
If you can **afford** something, you have enough money to pay for it. *I'm going to save up my pocket money until I can afford to buy some new skates.*

afraid
If you are **afraid**, you feel something nasty will happen to you. *Our dog is afraid of thunder.*

afternoon
Afternoon is the part of the day between morning and evening. *We go home from school at 3 o'clock in the afternoon.*

age
Your **age** is the number of years you have lived.

ago
Ago means at some time in the past. *The puppies were born only a week ago, so they are still tiny.*

agree *(agrees agreeing agreed)*
If somebody **agrees** with you, they think or feel the same way as you. *My brother and I never agree about what to watch on television.*

air
Air is what we breathe. **Air** is all around us, but we cannot see it. *We went for a walk in the fresh air.*

aircraft

An **aircraft** is any machine that can fly. Aeroplanes, gliders and helicopters are all different kinds of **aircraft**.

airport

An **airport** is a place with buildings and runways. Aircraft take off and land there, and people get on and off planes.

alarm

An **alarm** is something such as a bell or a flashing light that tells us that there is danger. *When they heard the fire alarm, everybody quickly left the building.*

album

1 An **album** is an empty book in which you can put such things as photos or stamps.
2 An **album** is also several different pieces of music together on a CD or tape.

alike

If two or more things or people are **alike**, they are the same in some way. *Lauren and her twin sister look so alike.*

alive

A person, plant or an animal that is **alive** is living and is not dead. *My great-grandma is still alive, but my great-granddad died last year.*

alligator

An **alligator** is an animal with a long tail, short legs and a large mouth with sharp teeth. **Alligators** are reptiles and live in rivers in some hot countries.

allow

(allows allowing allowed)
If you **allow** somebody to do something, you let them do it. *My mum doesn't allow me to watch television before school.*

almost

Almost means nearly, but not quite. *It's almost 4 o'clock.*

alone

If you are **alone**, there is nobody else with you. *Our dog gets upset if we leave her alone.*

aloud

Aloud means so that other people can hear. *The teacher read the story aloud to the class.*

alphabet

The **alphabet** is all the letters that we use to write words in a special order. The English **alphabet** starts with A and ends with Z.

always

1 **Always** means all the time. *You should always be kind to animals.*
2 **Always** also means every time. *Our dog is always pleased to see me when I get home from school.*

amazing

Something that is **amazing** surprises you very much. *I've got an amazing story to tell you.*

ambulance

An **ambulance** is a van or car that carries people to hospital when they are ill or hurt.

amount

An **amount** of something is how much there is. *Different sizes of container hold different amounts of food.*

amphibian

Amphibians are animals that live in water when they are young, and then live on land for most of the time when they are adults. Frogs, toads and newts are all kinds of **amphibians**.

ancient

Something that is **ancient** is very, very old.

angry *(angrier angriest)*

If you are **angry**, you are very cross. *Laura was angry when I let her hamster out of its cage.*

animal

An **animal** is anything that is alive and that can move from one place to another. Horses, tigers, elephants, birds, bees, fish and frogs are all **animals**.

ankle

Your **ankle** is the part of your leg where it joins your foot. *Lucy fell and hurt her ankle.*

anniversary (anniversaries)

An **anniversary** is a day that you remember because something important happened on that day in a past year. My aunt and uncle's wedding **anniversary** is on the 20th May.

annoy (annoys annoying annoyed)

If somebody **annoys** you, they make you cross by doing something you do not like. *It annoys me when my sister leaves her clothes lying all over the floor in our bedroom.*

another

Another means one more. *Have another sandwich.*

answer (answers answering answered)

1 When somebody speaks to you or asks you a question, you **answer** by speaking to them. *I asked him the time but he didn't answer.*
2 An **answer** is what you say to somebody who asks you a question. *Put up your hand if you know the answer.*

ant

An **ant** is a tiny insect. **Ants** live under the ground in groups called colonies.

apart

1 Apart means away from each other. *Jim planted the flowers 15 centimetres apart.*
2 Apart also means in pieces. *Tom took the clock apart to see how it worked and then he put it back together again.*

ape

An **ape** is a large animal that looks like a monkey, but without a tail. Gorillas and chimpanzees are all kinds of **apes**.

apologize (apologizes apologizing apologized)

When you **apologize** you say you are sorry about something you have said or done. *Kevin apologized for being late.*

appear (appears appearing appeared)

When something **appears** you begin to see it. *Tim suddenly appeared from behind the tree.*

apple

An **apple** is a round green, red or yellow fruit. **Apples** grow on trees.

area

An **area** is a part of a place. *Which area of town do you come from?*

argue (argues arguing argued)

If you **argue** with somebody, you talk in an angry way because you do not agree with them.

arm

Your **arms** are the parts of your body between your shoulders and your hands.

armour

Armour is a covering made of metal that soldiers wore long ago to protect themselves in battle.

army (armies)

An **army** is a large group of soldiers who are trained to fight together in wars.

arrive (arrives arriving arrived)

When you **arrive**, you get to a place. *What time does grandma's flight arrive?*

arrow

1 An **arrow** is a long thin stick with a point at one end. You shoot arrows from a bow.
2 An **arrow** is also a sign that shows the way.

art

Art is something special such as a painting, a drawing or a statue that somebody has made.

artist

An **artist** is a person who draws or paints pictures or makes other special and beautiful things.

ash *(ashes)*

Ash is the grey powder that you can see after something such as wood has burned.

ask *(asks asking asked)*

1 If you **ask** a question, you want to find the answer to something. *"Where is the railway station, please?" she asked.*
2 If you **ask** for something, you say you would like to have it. *Tamsin asked her brother to help her clean her bike.*

asleep

When you are **asleep**, you are sleeping. *I was asleep in bed when the telephone rang in the middle of the night and woke me up.*

assembly *(assemblies)*

Assembly is when a large group of people meet in one place. *We have school assembly every morning.*

astronaut

An **astronaut** is a person who travels in space.

ate Look at **eat**.
The baby ate all her breakfast.

atlas *(atlases)*

An **atlas** is a book of maps.

attack *(attacks attacking attacked)*

If somebody or something **attacks** you, they try to hurt you.

attention

1 When you pay **attention**, you listen and watch carefully.
2 If somebody or something attracts your **attention**, you notice them. *Rose tried to attract my attention by waving her umbrella.*

attic

An **attic** is a room inside the roof of a house.

attract *(attracts attracting attracted)*

1 If something **attracts** you, you notice it and become interested in it. *I was attracted by the poster in the shop window.*
2 Attract also means to make something come closer. *Brightly coloured flowers attract bees. A magnet attracts some kinds of metals.*

audience

An **audience** is a group of people who have come to a place to see or listen to something such as a film, play or piece of music.

aunt

Your **aunt** is your father's sister, your mother's sister or the wife of your uncle.

author

An **author** is a person who has written a book, play or poem.

automatic

A machine that is **automatic** can work on its own without a person looking after it. *Traffic lights are usually automatic.*

autumn

Autumn is the part of the year between summer and winter, when leaves fall off the trees.

awake

If you are **awake**, you are not asleep. *Owls stay awake at night to hunt for food.*

Bb

baby *(babies)*
A **baby** is a very young child.

back
1 The **back** is the part of a person or an animal between the neck and the bottom or tail.
2 The **back** of something is behind or opposite the front. *She left her bike at the back of the library.*

backwards
If you count **backwards** from 100, you start with 100 and finish with 1.

bad *(worse worst)*
1 Things that are **bad** are not good. *Too many sweets are bad for your teeth.*
2 Bad also means nasty or serious. *Megan has a bad cold so she isn't going to school today.*

bag
You use a **bag** to carry things in. **Bags** are made of paper, plastic, cloth or leather.

bake *(bakes baking baked)*
When you **bake** food, you cook it in an oven. *I am baking a chocolate cake for my uncle's birthday.*

balance *(balances balancing balanced)*
When you **balance** something, you keep it in place without letting it fall over. *Tara is balancing a book on her head very carefully.*

ball
A **ball** is a round thing that you use to play all kinds of games. *He kicked the ball into goal.*

ballet
Ballet is a special way of dancing. *Amy goes to ballet lessons on Saturdays.*

balloon
A **balloon** is a coloured bag made of rubber or plastic which you fill with gas or air to make it float. Some large **balloons** can float high in the sky and carry people in a special basket underneath.

banana
A **banana** is a long fruit with a yellow skin. **Bananas** grow in bunches on trees in hot countries.

band
1 A **band** is a group of people who play musical instruments together. *James plays the drums in the school band.*
2 A **band** is also a thin piece of material that you put around something. *He put a rubber band around the pens to keep them together.*

bang
A **bang** is a sudden loud noise. *The door blew shut with a bang.*

bank
1 A **bank** is a place that looks after money for people.
2 A **bank** is also the land along the sides of a lake or river.

bar
1 A **bar** is a long thin piece of metal. Animal cages have **bars**.
2 A **bar** is also a thick hard piece of something, such as a **bar** of soap or a **bar** of chocolate.

bare
1 Bare means without any clothes or anything else covering it. *She walks around the house in her bare feet.*
2 Bare also means empty. *The cupboard is bare.*

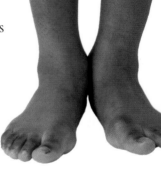

bark
1 A **bark** is the sudden noise that a dog makes. *Our dog has a very loud bark.*
2 Bark is also the rough covering on the trunk of a tree.

barn
A **barn** is a large building on a farm for keeping animals in or for storing things such as hay.

basket

You use a **basket** for carrying things in. **Baskets** are made of straw, strips of thin wood, or wire.

bat

1 A **bat** is an animal that looks like a mouse with wings. **Bats** hunt for food at night.

2 A **bat** is also a kind of wooden or metal stick. You use a **bat** for hitting the ball in games such as baseball or cricket.

bath

A **bath** is a large container that you fill with water and sit in to wash yourself all over.

bathroom

A **bathroom** is a room where you wash yourself. It has a bath or shower and sometimes it has a toilet as well.

battery *(batteries)*

A **battery** is something that stores electricity inside it. You put **batteries** in things like torches and toys to make them work.

battle

A **battle** is a fight between two armies or groups of people.

beach *(beaches)*

A **beach** is the land next to the sea. **Beaches** are covered with sand or small smooth stones called pebbles.

bead

A **bead** is a small round piece of glass, plastic or wood with a hole in it. You can put a string through the holes of a set of **beads** to make a necklace.

beak

A **beak** is the hard pointed part of a bird's mouth. Birds use their **beaks** to pick up food.

bean

A **bean** is a vegetable with a large seed inside that can be cooked and eaten. There are many different kinds of **bean**.

bear

A **bear** is a large wild animal with thick fur and sharp claws.

beard

A **beard** is the hair that grows on a man's chin.

beat *(beats beating beat beaten)*

1 If you **beat** something, you hit it again and again. *Tom is beating the drums.*

2 If you **beat** somebody in a game, you win and they lose.

beautiful

A **beautiful** thing is nice to look at, to hear or to smell.

beaver

A **beaver** is a furry animal that lives in or near lakes or rivers. It has a flat tail for swimming, and strong front teeth for chewing through wood.

bed

A **bed** is a piece of furniture that you lie on to sleep.

bee

A **bee** is a flying insect that can sting. **Bees** make honey.

beef

Beef is meat that comes from cattle. Hamburgers are made from **beef**.

beetle

A **beetle** is an insect with hard shiny wings. A ladybird is a kind of **beetle**.

begin *(begins beginning began begun)*

If you **begin** something, you start it. *You usually begin a book on the first page.*

behave *(behaves behaving behaved)*

The way we do things is how we **behave**. *The children behaved well and did not make too much noise.*

believe *(believes believing believed)*

If you **believe** something, you think it is true or real. *I don't believe in ghosts, do you?*

bell

A **bell** is something that makes a ringing sound when you hit it. Most **bells** are made of metal.

belong *(belongs belonging belonged)*

1 Something that **belongs** to you is yours. *Who does this funny hat belong to?*
2 If you **belong** to something, you are a part of it. *The twins belong to the football club.*

belt

A **belt** is a long strip of cloth or leather that you put around your waist. *You can use a belt to stop your trousers falling down.*

bench *(benches)*

A **bench** is a long seat that two or more people can sit on. *We sat on the park bench and fed the birds.*

bend *(bends bending bent)*

1 If you **bend** something, it stops being straight. *Henry bent the wire into a circle.*
2 If you **bend**, you move the top of your body downwards. *Sophie is bending down to pick something up from the floor.*

berry *(berries)*

A **berry** is a small fruit that grows on a bush. There are lots of different kinds of **berry** that are good to eat, such as strawberries, blackberries and raspberries. There are a few kinds of **berry** that are poisonous.

bicycle

A **bicycle** is a machine that you can ride on. **Bicycles** have two wheels and pedals. Bike is a short word for **bicycle**.

big *(bigger biggest)*

Something that is **big** is not small. Elephants are **big**.

bike Look at **bicycle**.

bird

A **bird** is an animal with feathers, wings and a beak. Most **birds** can fly. **Birds** lay eggs.

birthday

Your **birthday** is a day that you remember each year because it is the same day as the day you were born.

biscuit

A **biscuit** is a flat thin dry kind of cake.

bite *(bites biting bit bitten)*

When you **bite** something, you use your teeth to cut it. *Tom bit into the apple.*

blade

A **blade** is the sharp edge of a knife that can cut.

blame *(blames blaming blamed)*

If you **blame** somebody for something bad that happened, you think they did it. *Grandma blamed my dog for stealing the food from her shopping bag.*

blanket

A **blanket** is a large thick cover that keeps you warm in bed.

blew Look at **blow**.
Bart blew out the candles on the birthday cake.

blind

1 A person who is **blind** cannot see at all or cannot see very well.
2 A **blind** is a piece of material you pull down to cover a window.

blink *(blinks blinking blinked)*

When you **blink**, you close both your eyes and then open them again very quickly.

block

1 A **block** is a piece of something hard with flat sides, such as a **block** of wood or stone.
2 A **block** of flats is a large building with lots of flats.
3 *(blocks blocking blocked)*
When something **blocks** the way, other things or people cannot get through. *The broken-down lorry blocked the road.*

blood

Blood is the red liquid that your heart pumps round and round inside your body.

blow *(blows blowing blew blown)*
1 When you **blow**, you make air come out of your mouth. *The children are blowing up balloons.*
2 When the wind **blows**, it makes the air move.

blunt
If a knife or pencil is **blunt**, it is not sharp or pointed.

boat
A **boat** is something that carries people and things on water. There are many different kinds of **boat**, such as canoes and sailing boats.

body *(bodies)*
The **body** of a person or an animal is the whole of them. Snakes have very long **bodies**.

boil *(boils boiling boiled)*
When water **boils**, it gets very hot and you can see little bubbles and steam coming off it.

bone
Bones are the hard parts in the body of a person or an animal.

book
A **book** is made of pieces of paper fixed together between two covers. Most **books** have words and pictures inside. This dictionary is a **book**.

boot
1 A **boot** is a kind of shoe that covers your ankle and part of your leg.
2 A **boot** is also a place in a car where you can store things such as bags.

bored
If you are **bored**, you feel a bit cross or unhappy because you have nothing interesting to do.

born
When a baby is **born**, it begins life outside its mother's body. *The puppies were born last weekend.*

borrow *(borrows borrowing borrowed)*
If you **borrow** something from somebody, you take it to use for a short time before you give it back. *Can I borrow your pen for a moment, please?*

boss
The **boss** is the person who is in charge of other people.

bottle
A **bottle** is a container for liquids. **Bottles** are made of glass or plastic.

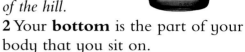

bottom
1 The **bottom** of something is the lowest part. *She got off her bike at the bottom of the hill.*
2 Your **bottom** is the part of your body that you sit on.

bought Look at **buy**.
Lily bought some bananas.

bounce *(bounces bouncing bounced)*
When something **bounces**, it springs back after hitting something hard. *Raj bounced the ball off the wall.*

bow
1 A **bow** is a special knot that you make with ribbon or string to decorate something. *Lisa is wearing a big blue bow in her hair.*
2 A **bow** is also a bent piece of wood with a string fixed from one end to the other. People use **bows** to shoot arrows.

bow *(bows bowing bowed)*
When you **bow**, you bend your body forward and down. *The knight bowed to the king.*

bowl
A **bowl** is a round deep dish for food or liquids.

box *(boxes)*

A **box** is a container for keeping things in. **Boxes** are made of cardboard, wood, plastic or sometimes metal.

boy

A **boy** is a male child. **Boys** grow up to be men.

brain

Your **brain** is inside your head. You use your **brain** to think and remember, and it sends messages to other parts of your body to control them.

branch *(branches)*

The **branches** of a tree grow out from its trunk like arms.

brave

If you are **brave**, you show that you are not afraid of something that is dangerous or frightening.

bread

Bread is a kind of food made from flour and baked in an oven.

break *(breaks breaking broke broken)*

If something **breaks**, it goes into pieces or stops working. *I dropped the glass and it broke. Our iron has broken - it doesn't get hot any more.*

breakfast

Breakfast is the first meal that you eat in the day. *I had an egg for breakfast this morning.*

breathe *(breathes breathing breathed)*

When you **breathe**, you take air into your body through your nose and mouth and let it out again. *You breathe faster when you run.*

brick

A **brick** is a block of clay that has been baked so it is very hard and strong. A lot of houses are built of **bricks**.

bridge

A **bridge** is built over a river, railway or road so that people can get across.

bright

1 Something that is **bright** gives out a lot of light and shines strongly. *You should never look straight at the sun because its light is so bright it will hurt your eyes.*
2 Colours that are **bright** are clear and easy to see and are not pale or light.
3 Somebody who is **bright** is clever and learns quickly.

bring *(brings bringing brought)*

Bring means to carry or take somebody or something with you. *Bring that chair over here please. Matt brought a friend to the party.*

broke, broken

Look at **break**.
Ben broke the window. Lucy has broken her leg.

broom

A **broom** is a kind of large brush with a long handle. We use **brooms** for sweeping floors and paths.

brother

Your **brother** is a boy or man who has the same mother and father as you.

brought Look at **bring**.
I have brought you a present.

brush *(brushes)*

A **brush** is a tool with a lot of stiff hairs called bristles. You use a toothbrush to clean your teeth and another kind of **brush** for sweeping the floor.

bubble

A **bubble** is a light floating ball of liquid or soap filled with air.

bucket

A **bucket** is a container with a handle. You use it for carrying things. **Buckets** are made of metal or plastic.

bud

A **bud** is a flower or leaf on a plant, just before it opens.

bug

A **bug** is an insect. Ants and bees are **bugs**.

build *(builds building built)*

When you **build** something, you make it by putting different parts together. *My baby sister is building a tower out of wooden blocks.*

building

Buildings are things like houses, factories, schools, shops and blocks of flats. All **buildings** have walls and a roof.

bulb

1 A **bulb** is the round part of some plants that grow under the ground. *Daffodils grow from bulbs.*

2 A **bulb** is also the round glass part of a lamp that gives light.

bull

A **bull** is the male of the cattle family. A cow is the female.

bulldozer

A **bulldozer** is a kind of big tractor that moves rocks, earth and other things to make the land flat, ready for building on.

burn *(burns burning burned or burnt)*

1 Something that is **burning** is on fire.

2 If you **burn** something, you damage it with fire. *Don't touch the oven or you'll burn yourself.*

burst *(bursts bursting burst)*

If something **bursts**, it breaks apart suddenly. *The balloon burst with a loud bang.*

bury *(buries burying buried)*

If you **bury** something, you put it in the ground and cover it. *The dog buried its bone in the garden.*

busy *(busier busiest)*

1 If you are **busy**, you have a lot of things to do. *I've been busy all day making food for the party.*

2 If a place is **busy**, a lot of things are happening there. *The streets of the city are always crowded and very busy.*

butter

Butter is a yellow food that is made from cream. *I spread butter on my bread.*

butterfly *(butterflies)*

A **butterfly** is an insect with white or brightly coloured wings. **Butterflies** grow from caterpillars.

bunch *(bunches)*

A **bunch** is a group of things that are fixed or tied together. *We bought a bunch of bananas, and a bunch of flowers for grandma.*

bus *(buses)*

A **bus** is a large vehicle with rows of seats inside for carrying a lot of people from one place to another on short journeys.

bush *(bushes)*

A **bush** is a small low tree with a lot of branches. Roses and berries grow on **bushes**.

business *businesses*

A **business** is a group of people who work together to make or sell things.

button

A **button** is a small round thing on clothes. Shirts and jackets have **buttons** to keep them done up.

buy *(buys buying bought)*

When you **buy** something, you give money to have it. *Mum bought me some new shoes for school when we went shopping.*

buzz *(buzzes buzzing buzzed)*

If something **buzzes**, it makes a sound like a bee.

Cc

cabbage

A **cabbage** is a round vegetable with lots of big green leaves.

cabin

1 A **cabin** is a small house. **Cabins** are often made of wood. *We stayed in a log cabin in the woods.*
2 A **cabin** is also a room on a ship, or the part of an aircraft where people sit.

cage

A **cage** is a kind of box for keeping animals in. The sides are made of metal bars. *My pet mice live in a cage.*

cake

A **cake** is a sweet food that is made from butter, eggs, sugar and flour, and baked in an oven.

calculator

A **calculator** is a small machine that can work out sums quickly. You make it work by pressing buttons.

calendar

A **calendar** shows all the days, weeks and months of a year.

calf *(calves)*

A **calf** is a young cow or bull. A young elephant or a young whale is also called a **calf**.

call *(calls calling called)*

1 If you **call** somebody, you shout to tell them to come to you. *"Dinner's ready," she called from downstairs.*
2 **Call** also means to use the telephone. *I'll call you this evening at about seven.*
3 When you are **called** something, you have that name. *The black and white kitten is called Archie.*

calm

If you are **calm**, you are not afraid or excited. *If you see a snake in the jungle, it's very important to try to stay calm.*

camel

A **camel** is a large animal with a long neck and either one or two humps on its back. **Camels** can go for a long time without water. They are used for carrying people and things in the desert.

camera

A **camera** is a thing that you use for taking photos.

camp

A **camp** is a place where people live or stay in tents.

can

A **can** is a metal container. You can buy a lot of different kinds of food and drink in **cans.**

candle

A **candle** is a stick of wax with a piece of string called a wick through the middle. As the wick burns, the **candle** gives light.

cap

1 A **cap** is a small soft hat with a stiff part called a peak at the front.
2 A **cap** is also a small lid. *Make sure you put the cap back on the toothpaste when you've finished using it.*

car

A **car** is a machine that you travel in on roads. A **car** has four wheels and an engine. It can usually carry four or five people.

card

1 **Cards** are thick pieces of paper with words or pictures on them. People send postcards to their friends when they go on holiday. On your birthday, people send you birthday **cards**.
2 You use special **cards** with numbers and pictures on them for playing games.

cardboard

Cardboard is thick strong paper. Some boxes and cartons are made of **cardboard**.

care (cares caring cared)

1 When you **care** for somebody or something, you look after them. *Ned cared for the injured rabbit until it was better.*

2 When you **care** about something, you think it is important. *The only thing my sister cares about is football!*

careful

If you are **careful**, you think about what you are doing and try to do it well and safely without making mistakes. *You can carry those plates but be careful you don't drop them.*

careless

A person who is **careless** makes mistakes because they are not thinking about what they are doing. *Careless drivers can easily cause accidents.*

carpet

A **carpet** is a large thick cover for a floor.

carrot

A **carrot** is a long vegetable that is orange in colour. **Carrots** grow under the ground.

carry (carries carrying carried)

When you **carry** something, you hold it and take it somewhere. *Charlie carried the box very carefully.*

cart

A **cart** is a wooden vehicle with two or four wheels that can be pulled along by a horse or pushed by a person.

carton

A **carton** is a box made of plastic or cardboard. You can buy many kinds of food and drink in **cartons**. *We bought a carton of orange juice.*

cartoon

1 A **cartoon** is a funny drawing in a newspaper.

2 A **cartoon** is also a short film using drawings that seem to move. *They show a lot of really good cartoons on television.*

carve (carves carving carved)

When somebody **carves** wood or stone, they make a shape from it by cutting it.

case

1 A **case** is a container for keeping or carrying things in. *I put my camera in its case so that it didn't get damaged.*

2 A **case** is also a bag that you carry your clothes in when you go on holiday. *Have you packed your case yet?*

cash

Cash is money in coins and notes. *Mum paid by cheque because she didn't have any cash.*

cassette

A **cassette** is a flat plastic box with tape inside that plays and records music and sometimes pictures. *a video cassette, a music cassette.*

castle

A **castle** is a big building with thick walls and high towers. **Castles** were built long ago to keep the people inside safe in times of war.

cat

A **cat** is a small furry animal with a long tail and sharp claws. Many people keep **cats** as pets. Some kinds of large **cats** such as lions and tigers are wild animals.

catch (catches catching caught)

1 When you **catch** something, you take hold of it as it moves towards you. *Tom threw a stick and his dog caught it.*

2 If you **catch** an illness from somebody, you get it too. *I think I've caught your cold.*

3 If you **catch** a train or bus, you get on it to go somewhere. *We must hurry up because we've got a train to catch.*

caterpillar

A **caterpillar** looks like a furry worm with lots of legs. **Caterpillars** turn into butterflies and moths.

cattle

Cattle are cows and bulls on a farm. Farmers keep **cattle** for their meat and milk.

caught Look at catch.

I threw the ball and Emily caught it.

cause *(causes causing caused)*

If you **cause** something, you make it happen. *Her careless driving caused the accident.*

cave

A **cave** is a big hole in the side of a mountain or under the ground.

ceiling

A **ceiling** is the top part of a room, above your head. *Mum climbed up the ladder and began to paint the ceiling.*

centre

The **centre** of something is the middle part of it. *The flower has yellow petals and a black centre.*

centre

century *(centuries)*

A **century** lasts for exactly one hundred years.

cereal

A **cereal** is a kind of food that people eat for breakfast. **Cereals** are made from the seeds of plants such as rice and wheat.

chain

A **chain** is made of a line of metal rings joined together.

chair

A **chair** is a piece of furniture that one person can sit on. A **chair** has a seat and a back.

chalk

Chalk is soft, white rock. You can write with a stick of **chalk**.

champion

A **champion** is a person who has won a game or sports competition. *Callum is the school swimming champion this year.*

change *(changes changing changed)*

1 When something **changes**, it becomes different in some way. *The traffic lights changed from red to green. Caterpillars change into moths or butterflies.*

2 If you **change** your clothes, you put on something different. *I change out of my school uniform as soon as I get home.*

channel

1 A **channel** is a narrow sea between two pieces of land.
2 A television set has different **channels** that you can choose from. Each **channel** has different programmes.

charge

1 If you are in **charge** of something, it is your job to look after it. *Dad left me in charge of my little brother while he was cleaning his car.*
2 *(charges charging charged)* If somebody **charges** you for something, they are asking you to pay money for it.

chase *(chases chasing chased)*

If you **chase** somebody or something, you run after them to try to catch them. *The cat chased after the ball of wool.*

cheap

If something is **cheap**, it does not cost a lot of money.

check *(checks checking checked)*

When you **check** something, you make sure that it is right. *James checked his spelling carefully.*

cheek
Your **cheeks** are the two soft parts on each side of your face, under your eyes.

cheerful
If you are **cheerful**, you are happy and you smile a lot.

cheese
Cheese is a food made from milk. There are many different kinds of **cheese**.

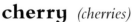

cherry (cherries)
A **cherry** is a small round fruit with a hard seed called a stone in the middle. **Cherries** grow on trees.

chest
1 Your **chest** is the front part of your body between your shoulders and your stomach.
2 A **chest** is also a strong heavy box with a lid.
The jewellery filled the wooden chest.

chew (chews chewing chewed)
When you **chew** food, you keep biting it to make it soft. *The dog was chewing a bone.*

chick
A **chick** is a very young bird.

chicken
A **chicken** is a bird that people keep for its eggs and for its meat.

child (children)
A **child** is a young boy or girl. **Children** grow up to be men and women.

chimney (chimneys)
A **chimney** is a tall pipe above a fire inside a building. A **chimney** lets smoke escape to the outside.

chin
Your **chin** is the bottom part of your face under your mouth.

chocolate
Chocolate is a sweet brown food or drink.

choose (chooses choosing chose chosen)
When you **choose** something, you decide which one you want. *Mum let us choose what we wanted for dinner.*

chop (chops chopping chopped)
If you **chop** something, you cut it into small pieces with an axe or a knife. *Jenny chopped the carrots.*

circus (circuses)
A **circus** is a show with acrobats and clowns that you go to watch in a big tent. **Circuses** travel around from place to place.

city (cities)
A **city** is a very big town. New York and Paris are **cities**.

clap (claps clapping clapped)
When you **clap**, you make a noise by hitting your hands together. You **clap** to show that you have enjoyed something.

class (classes)
A **class** is a group of pupils who are learning together. *How many children are there in your class at school?*

claw
Claws are the sharp curved nails on the feet of birds, cats and many other animals.

clay
Clay is a special kind of mud that is used for making things such as pots and bricks. **Clay** becomes hard when it dries.

clean
1 Something that is **clean** is not dirty. *My hands are clean.*
2 (cleans cleaning cleaned) When you **clean** something, you take the dirt off it. *Carol cleaned the windows.*

clear
1 If something is **clear**, you can see through it easily. *Today the water is so clear I can see right to the bottom of the pond.*
2 **Clear** also means easy to understand, to see or to hear. *These instructions are very clear.*

clever

A **clever** person or animal learns and understands things quickly.

cliff

A **cliff** is a hill with one side that goes almost straight down. Most **cliffs** are by the sea.

climb *(climbs climbing climbed)*

When you **climb**, you use your hands and feet to go up or down something. *Be careful when you climb the ladder.*

clock

A **clock** is a machine that shows you what time it is.

close *(closes closing closed)*

When you **close** something, you shut it. *Please close all the windows before you go out. We closed our eyes and counted to ten.*

close

If something is **close**, it is near. *The park is close to the hospital.*

cloth

Cloth is material that clothes are made of. A lot of **cloth** is made of wool or cotton.

clothes

Clothes are the things that people wear to cover their bodies such as jeans and jumpers.

cloud

A **cloud** is a white or grey shape floating high in the sky. **Clouds** are made of millions and millions of drops of water.

clown

A **clown** is a funny person in a circus who dresses in strange clothes and makes people laugh.

clue

A **clue** is something that helps us to find the answer to a problem or puzzle. *I'll give you a clue what's in the box. It's got hands and a face, but no arms or legs. It's a clock!*

coach *(coaches)*

1 A **coach** is a bus that carries people on long journeys.
2 A **coach** is also a person who teaches people to play a game such as tennis or football.

coast

The **coast** is the land near the sea. *They live on the coast.*

coat

You wear a **coat** over your other clothes to keep you warm when you go outside. **Coats** have long sleeves and they are usually made of thick cloth.

coffee

Coffee is a drink that you make by adding hot water to a brown powder. The powder is made from the beans of the **coffee** bush.

coin

A **coin** is a piece of money made of metal. **Coins** are often round.

cold

1 Cold means not hot or warm. *In this country, the weather can become very cold in the winter.*
2 If you have a **cold**, you are ill and you sneeze a lot.

collar

1 A **collar** is the part of a shirt, jacket or coat that fits around your neck.
2 A **collar** is also a strip of leather or cloth that goes around the neck of a dog or cat.

collect *(collects collecting collected)*

1 When you **collect** things, you save a lot of them because you find them interesting. *Edward collects comics as a hobby.*
2 When you **collect** somebody from a place, you go there to fetch them. *Dad usually collects us from school on Mondays.*

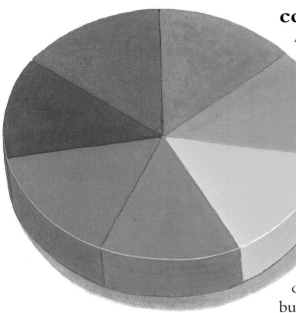

colour
Red, blue, yellow, purple and green are **colours.** *What is your favourite colour?*

comfortable
If something is **comfortable**, it is nice to be in or to wear. *This armchair is very comfortable to sleep in.*

comic
A **comic** is a kind of newspaper with cartoons and drawings that tell stories.

compact disc
A **compact disc** is a round flat silver-coloured piece of plastic with music or other sounds stored on it. It is also called a CD.

competition
A **competition** is a game or test to see who is the best at doing something. *I won first prize in the story-writing competition.*

computer
A **computer** is a machine that stores information and can work out many kinds of things very quickly. Some **computers** are used to control other machines, or to build things.

container
A **container** is something that you can put other things into. Boxes, bottles, cans and jars are all **containers**.

control *(controls controlling controlled)*
If you **control** somebody or something, you make it do what you want it to do. *You control a kite with long pieces of string.*

cook *(cooks cooking cooked)*
When you **cook** food, you make it ready to eat by using heat. You **cook** food in a cooker, or on top of it. *My dad is cooking the dinner tonight.*

cool
Something that is **cool** is quite cold. *Would you like a cool drink of lemonade or water?*

copy *(copies copying copied)*
If you **copy** something, you make it exactly the same as something else. *Darren copies everything his big brother does.*

corn
Corn is plants such as wheat that are grown for their seeds and made into flour.

corner
A **corner** is where two straight lines or edges meet. *A square has four corners.*

correct
Something that is **correct** has no mistakes. *He gave the correct answers to all the questions.*

cost *(costs costing cost)*
What something **costs** is how much money you have to pay for it. *How much does it cost to get into the zoo?*

costume
Costumes are the clothes that actors wear in plays or the clothes that people in a country wear at special times.

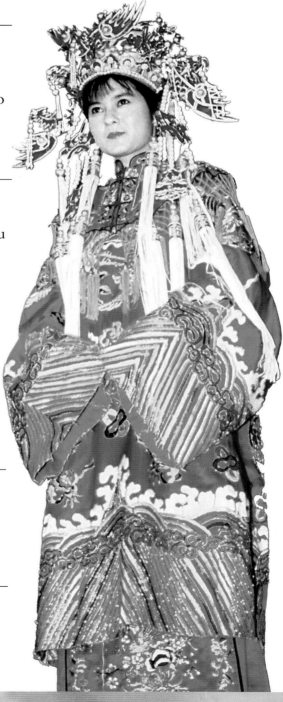

cot

A **cot** is a bed with high sides for a baby or young child.

cottage

A **cottage** is a small house. Most **cottages** are in the country.

cotton

1 **Cotton** is a light cloth made from **cotton** plants. Shirts and dresses can be made from **cotton**.
2 **Cotton** is also thread that you use for sewing.

cough (coughs coughing coughed)

When you **cough**, you make a sudden loud noise in your throat.

count (counts counting counted)

1 When you **count**, you say numbers in the right order. *Count from one to ten.*
2 **Count** also means to find how many.

country

1 A **country** is a part of the world with its own people and laws. France is a **country**.
2 The **country** is the land away from towns.

cousin

Your **cousin** is the son or daughter of your uncle or aunt.

cover (covers covering covered)

If you **cover** something, you put something else over it.

cow

A **cow** is a large farm animal that gives us milk.

crack

A **crack** is a thin line along something that has broken but that has not fallen to pieces. *Can you see the crack in this plate?*

crane

A **crane** is a machine that can move and lift very heavy things.

crash (crashes crashing crashed)

When something **crashes**, it hits or falls on to something else with a loud noise. *The bull crashed through the wooden fence.*

crawl (crawls crawling crawled)

If you **crawl**, you move along on your hands and knees. Babies often **crawl** before they can walk.

crayon

A **crayon** is a soft pencil made of coloured wax for drawing.

cream

Cream is the thick yellow part at the top of milk. *Would you like some cream on your cake?*

creature

A **creature** is any animal. *We watched a film about strange creatures from Mars.*

creep (creeps creeping crept)

When something **creeps**, it moves along slowly and quietly. *We crept upstairs so that we wouldn't wake anyone. The cat is creeping towards the bird.*

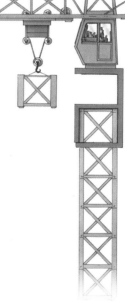

crew

A **crew** is a group of people who work together, especially on a boat, an aeroplane or a spacecraft. *The crew of the spaceship sent a message to Earth.*

cricket

1 **Cricket** is a game played with bats and a ball by two teams of eleven people.
2 A **cricket** is a jumping insect that makes a sound by rubbing its wings together.

curl

A **curl** is a piece of hair in a curved shape. Some people have straight hair and other people have curly hair.

crocodile

A **crocodile** is a large reptile with a long body. It has a huge mouth with sharp teeth. **Crocodiles** live in rivers in some hot countries.

crooked

Something that is **crooked** is bent and not straight. *A crooked branch.*

crop

Crops are plants that farmers grow as food.

cross

1 If you are **cross**, you feel a bit angry.
2 *(crosses)* A **cross** is a mark like + or X.
3 *(crosses crossing crossed)* If you **cross** something such as a road, you go from one side to the other. *We crossed the river in a boat.*

crowd

A **crowd** is a lot of people together in one place. *A large crowd of people were on the road.*

crowded

If a place is **crowded** it is full of people. *A crowded shopping centre.*

crown

A **crown** is a kind of hat made of gold or silver that kings and queens wear.

cruel *(crueller cruellest)*

People who hurt other people or animals on purpose are **cruel**.

crumb

A **crumb** is a tiny piece of bread or cake.

cry *(cries crying cried)*

When you **cry**, tears come out of your eyes. *My little sister always cries when she falls over.*

cub

A **cub** is a young bear, fox, lion, tiger or wolf.

cuddle *(cuddles cuddling cuddled)*

When you **cuddle** somebody you put your arms around them and hold them.

cup

A **cup** is a small bowl with a handle that you drink out of.

cupboard

A **cupboard** is a piece of furniture with doors and shelves for keeping things in.

curtain

Curtains are pieces of cloth that hang at the sides of a window and that you pull across to cover the window.

curve *(curves curving curved)*

When a line bends one way, it **curves**. *The road curves to the left a little way further on.*

cushion

A **cushion** is a kind of big soft bag that you put on a chair to make it more comfortable.

cut *(cuts cutting cut)*

1 When you **cut** something, you use a knife or scissors. *Kyle cut the pizza into six pieces. Harry had his hair cut.*
2 If you **cut** yourself, you hurt yourself on something sharp. *Kathy cut her finger on a very sharp piece of glass.*

Dd

damage *(damages damaging damaged)*
If you **damage** something, you break it or spoil it in some way. *The box got damaged when I dropped it on the floor.*

damp
If something is **damp**, it is a little wet. *Use a damp cloth to clean the table top.*

dance *(dances dancing danced)*
When you **dance**, you move your body about to music.

danger
Danger is something bad that might happen.

dangerous
If something is **dangerous**, it might hurt you. *It is dangerous to swim in the river.*

dark
1 When it is **dark**, there is no light. *It is dark at night.*

2 **Dark** colours are colours such as brown and black. *Elinor has very dark hair.*

darts
Darts are small arrows that you throw at a round board in a game called **darts**.

date
A **date** is the day, month and year when something happens. *What's the date today?*

daughter
A **daughter** is a girl or woman who is somebody's child.

day
1 A **day** is the 24 hours between midnight and the next midnight. There are seven **days** in a week.
2 **Day** is also the time when it is light outside. *Owls sleep when it is day and go hunting at night.*

dead
If somebody or something is **dead**, it is not alive any more.

deaf
A person who is **deaf** cannot hear well or cannot hear at all. Some **deaf** people make signs with their hands as a way of talking to one another.

dear
1 If something is **dear**, it costs a lot of money. *These rollerblades are too dear - let's look for a cheaper pair.*
2 If somebody or something is **dear** to you, you love them.
3 You put **Dear** before a person's name when you write a letter.

decide *(decides deciding decided)*
When you **decide**, you make up your mind about something. *Jade is trying to decide which dress to wear.*

decorate *(decorates decorating decorated)*
When you **decorate** something, you add things to it to make it look prettier. *Sarah is decorating the birthday cake.*

decoration
A **decoration** is a thing that has been added to make something look nicer.

deep
Something that is **deep** goes down a very long way. *We dug a deep hole to plant the tree in.*

deer
A **deer** is a wild animal that can run fast. Male **deer** have horns called antlers.

delicious
Something that is **delicious** is very good to eat or smell. *These apples are delicious.*

delighted

If you are **delighted**, you are very pleased about something. *Sue was delighted with her new bike.*

deliver *(delivers delivering delivered)*

If somebody **delivers** something to you, they bring it to you. *Dominic delivered the party invitations to his friends.*

dentist

A **dentist** is a person who looks after people's teeth.

describe *(describes describing described)*

If you **describe** something, you say or write what it is like. *Can you describe the strange bird you saw?*

desert

A **desert** is land where there is very little rain and where few plants can grow.

design

If you **design** something, you make a sketch or plan to show what it is going to look like when it is made.

desk

A **desk** is a table where you sit to read or write. Some **desks** have drawers.

dessert

Dessert is the sweet food that you eat at the end of a meal. *Billy had ice-cream for dessert and the rest of us had fruit salad.*

destroy *(destroys destroying destroyed)*

If something is **destroyed**, it is damaged or broken so badly that it cannot be used again. *The factory was destroyed by fire.*

detective

A **detective** is a person who looks for clues and tries to find out who did something such as a robbery.

diamond

A **diamond** is a shiny jewel that is clear like glass. **Diamonds** are expensive. *He bought his wife a diamond ring for her birthday.*

diary *(diaries)*

A **diary** is a book with a space for each day where you can write down important things that happen or are going to happen on that day.

dice

Dice are small blocks with a different number of dots on each side. You use **dice** for playing games.

dictionary *(dictionaries)*

A **dictionary** is a book that has a list of words from A to Z. You use a **dictionary** to check meanings and spellings.

die *(dies dying died)*

If somebody or something **dies**, they stop living. *Our dog was very old when she died.*

different

Different means not the same. *These houses are different in twelve ways. Can you see how?*

difficult

If something is **difficult**, it is not easy to do or to understand. *It's very difficult to balance for a long time on one leg.*

dig *(digs digging dug)*

When you **dig**, you move soil or sand to make a hole in the ground. *We dug a big hole on the beach.*

dinner

Dinner is the main meal of the day. Some people eat **dinner** in the middle of the day, and other people eat it in the evening.

dinosaur

A **dinosaur** is a reptile that lived millions of years ago. There were many different kinds of **dinosaurs** such as the Ultrasaurus in the picture. This **dinosaur** ate plants. Some kinds of **dinosaurs** were very strong and fierce.

dip *(dips dipping dipped)*

If you **dip** something in a liquid, you put it in quickly and take it out again. *She dipped her finger in the melted chocolate and tasted it.*

direction

A **direction** is the way you go or the way something points. *They walked in the direction of the town.*

dirt
Dirt is dust, mud or anything that makes things not clean.

dirty *(dirtier dirtiest)*
If something is **dirty**, it is covered in dirt. *Our dog always gets really dirty when we take her for a walk in the park.*

disappear
(disappears disappearing disappeared)
If somebody or something **disappears**, they go away and you cannot see them any more. *The bus disappeared over the hill.*

disappoint *(disappoints disappointing disappointed)*
If you are **disappointed**, you are sad because something you were hoping for did not happen. *Mark was disappointed because he didn't win the prize.*

disaster
A **disaster** is something very bad that happens and that may hurt a lot of people. Floods and earthquakes are **disasters**.

discover *(discovers discovering discovered)*
If you **discover** something, you find it or learn about it for the first time.

disguise
A **disguise** is something that you wear to change how you look.

dish *(dishes)*
A **dish** is a bowl for putting food in. *Our dog has her own dish.*

distance
Distance is how far two places are from one another. We can measure **distance** in miles or kilometres. *It's a short distance from our house to the school.*

disturb *(disturbs disturbing disturbed)*
If you **disturb** somebody, you stop them doing what they are doing, by making a noise or speaking to them. *Don't disturb Dad while he is on the telephone.*

dive *(dives diving dived)*
When you **dive**, you jump into water with your arms and head first.

divide *(divides dividing divided)*
1 When you **divide** something, you make it into smaller parts. *We divided the pizza into six pieces.*
2 When you **divide** numbers, you find out how many times one number goes into another number. *Ten divided by five is two.*

dizzy *(dizzier dizziest)*
When you are **dizzy**, you feel that things are spinning around you and that you are going to fall over. *I felt a bit dizzy when I got off the roundabout at the fair.*

doctor
A **doctor** is a person who helps you get better when you are ill. **Doctors** sometimes give you medicine or pills.

dog
Dogs are animals that people keep as pets or to do work. *The blind woman in our street has a dog who helps her find her way.*

doll
A **doll** is a toy that looks like a small person.

dolphin
A **dolphin** is an animal that lives in the sea. **Dolphins** are intelligent and friendly.

donkey
A **donkey** is an animal that looks like a small horse. **Donkeys** have long ears.

door
You open a **door** to go into a room or building. Things such as cars and cupboards also have **doors** that you open and close.

dot
A **dot** is a small round mark.

double
Double means twice as much or twice as many of something. *I had a double helping of ice-cream.*

drag *(drags dragging dragged)*
If you **drag** something, you pull it along the ground slowly. *We dragged the heavy box across the floor.*

dragon
A **dragon** is a kind of monster that you can read about in stories. **Dragons** have wings and a long tail and they breathe fire.

drain
A **drain** is a pipe that takes water away. *When you have finished having a bath, you take out the plug and the water goes down the drain.*

drank
Look at **drink**. *My brother drank all the orange juice.*

draw
(draws drawing drew drawn) When you **draw**, you make a picture of something with a pencil, pen or crayon.

drawer
A **drawer** is a kind of box that slides in and out of a piece of furniture. You use a **drawer** for keeping things in.

dream
A **dream** is pictures and thoughts that go through your head when you are asleep. *Last night I had a dream that I was a famous ballet dancer.*

dress
1 *(dresses)* A **dress** is something that girls and women wear. It has a top joined to a skirt. *She wore a pink party dress.*
2 *(dresses dressing dressed)* When you **dress**, you put your clothes on your body.

drew
Look at **draw**. *Look what I drew at school today.*

drill
A **drill** is a tool for making holes in things such as walls and pieces of wood.

drink
(drinks drinking drank drunk) When you **drink**, you take liquid into your mouth and down into your stomach. *Can I have something to drink?*

drip
(drips dripping dripped) When liquid **drips**, it falls in drops. *The paint dripped all over the floor and made a mess.*

drive
(drives driving drove driven) When somebody **drives** something such as a car, bus or train, they control it and make it move along. *My uncle drives a lorry up and down the motorway.*

drop
1 A **drop** is a very small amount of a liquid.
2 *(drops dropping dropped)* If you **drop** something, you let it fall to the ground by accident. *Tom dropped the game on the floor and the pieces went everywhere.*

drown
(drowns drowning drowned) If somebody **drowns**, they die because they are under water where they cannot breathe.

drum
A **drum** is a musical instrument that you play by beating it with your hands or with a stick.

drunk
Look at **drink**. *Somebody has drunk my milk.*

dry
1 *(drier driest)* If something is **dry**, it is not wet.
2 *(dries drying dried)* If you **dry** something, you make it dry. *Jo used a hair drier to dry her hair.*

duck
A **duck** is a bird that lives near water and can swim.

dug
Look at **dig**. *Our dog dug a hole in the garden.*

dungeon
A **dungeon** is an underground prison in a castle.

dust
Dust is tiny dry pieces of dirt-like powder. *The furniture in the old man's house was covered in dust.*

duvet
A **duvet** is a thick warm cover for a bed.

Ee

earthquake
An **earthquake** happens when the ground shakes. **Earthquakes** can make buildings fall down.

east
East is the direction where the Sun rises in the morning. **East** is the opposite of west.

easy *(easier easiest)*
Something that is **easy** is not hard to do or to understand. *This machine is easy to use.*

eat *(eats eating ate eaten)*
When you **eat**, you put food in your mouth and it goes down into your stomach.

echo *(echoes)*
An **echo** is a sound that bounces back from something so that you can hear it again. *She clapped her hands in the cave and then listened for the echo.*

edge
The **edge** of something is its end or side. *Don't go too near the edge of the cliff.*

egg
Eggs are oval things with thin shells where baby birds, reptiles and fish grow until they are ready to hatch. Many people eat the **eggs** that hens lay.

elbow
Your **elbow** is the part of your arm where it bends.

electricity
Electricity is a kind of power that travels along wires. It gives us light and heat and makes many kinds of machine work.

elephant
An **elephant** is a very large animal. It has large ears, a long nose called a trunk, and two huge teeth called tusks.

eagle
An **eagle** is a large bird with strong claws and a curved beak. **Eagles** catch small animals and eat other birds.

ear
Your **ears** are the two parts, one on each side of your head, that you use for hearing.

early *(earlier earliest)*
1 If you get somewhere **early**, you get there before the usual time. *We arrived at the party early to help blow up balloons.*
2 Early also means near the beginning of something. *Mum gets home from work in the early evening.*

earn *(earns earning earned)*
If you **earn** money, you get money for work that you do.

earth
1 The **Earth** is the planet that we live on. It has a round shape.
2 The ground where plants grow is called **earth**. *We dug a hole in the earth.*

emerald
An **emerald** is a green jewel. **Emeralds** cost a lot of money. *She wore an emerald necklace.*

empty (emptier emptiest)

If something is **empty**, there is nothing inside it. *His glass is empty. Can you fill it up please?*

end

1 The **end** of something is the last part of it, where it stops. *Take the end of the rope and pull.*

2 *(ends ending ended)* When something **ends**, it finishes. *When the film ended I went to bed.*

enemy (enemies)

An **enemy** is a person who does not like you and wants to hurt you in some way.

energy

Energy is power that makes things work. **Energy** from electricity, gas and water gives us light and heat, and makes machines work. We use our body's **energy** when we jump and run.

engine

An **engine** is a machine that uses energy to make things move. Cars and buses have **engines**.

engine

enjoy (enjoys enjoying enjoyed)

If you **enjoy** something, you like doing it. *I enjoy swimming and playing the piano.*

enormous

Something that is **enormous** is very big. *Some dinosaurs that once lived on the Earth were enormous.*

enough

When you have **enough** of something, you have as much or as many as you need. *Do you have enough money to buy that book?*

enter (enters entering entered)

If you **enter** a place, you go in. *She entered the house by the back door.*

entrance

An **entrance** is the way into a building. *The entrance to the swimming baths is on the left-hand side of the building.*

envelope

An **envelope** is a paper cover for a letter. *She put her letter inside the yellow envelope and then posted it.*

environment

The **environment** is everything that is around us, especially the air, sea, plants and animals. *It is very important that we take care of the environment.*

equal

1 Things that are **equal** are the same in size, number or weight. *One metre is equal to one hundred centimetres.*

2 *(equals, equalling, equalled)* If one thing **equals** another, they are the same size or number. *Three plus two equals five.*

equipment

Equipment is all the things that you need to do something. *You need special equipment if you want to play tennis.*

escape (escapes escaping escaped)

When you **escape**, you get away from somebody or something. *The parrot escaped from its cage.*

especially

Especially means more than others or more than anything else. *I love all kinds of cakes, especially chocolate cake.*

even

1 Something that is **even** is smooth and flat. *Spread an even layer of icing on top of the cake.*

2 **Even** can mean equal. *At half time the scores were even.*

3 **Even** numbers are numbers that can be divided by two and leave nothing over. *Two, four, sixty and one hundred are even numbers.*

evening

Evening is the part of the day between afternoon and night, before you go to bed.

eventually

Eventually means in the end. *We got lost and then the car broke down, but we got home eventually.*

evil

A person who is **evil** is very bad or cruel. *I read a story about an evil wizard.*

evergreen

An **evergreen** tree or plant keeps its leaves all the year round. Ivy is an **evergreen** plant.

excellent

Excellent means very, very good.

except

Except means leaving out somebody or something. *Alfie has eaten everything except the cabbage.*

excited

If you are **excited**, you are so happy and interested in something that you cannot keep quiet or think about anything else. *Jamal is very excited about going to America for his holidays.*

excuse

An **excuse** is what you say to tell people why you have or have not done something. *What excuse did you give your teacher for being late again?*

exercise

1 **Exercises** are movements such as jumping, running and touching your toes that you do to make your body stronger.
2 An **exercise** is a piece of work that you do to help you learn something. *Our teacher asked us to do some exercises from our maths book.*

exit

An **exit** is the way out of a building.

expect *(expects expecting expected)*

If you **expect** something to happen, you think that it will. *I expect grandma will take us to the park at the weekend.*

expensive

Something that is **expensive** costs a lot of money. *The jewellery was very expensive.*

explain *(explains explaining explained)*

When you **explain** something to somebody, you tell them about it so that they can understand it. *Dad explained how an engine works.*

explode *(explodes exploding exploded)*

When something **explodes**, it bursts into small pieces with a loud bang. *The fireworks exploded above our heads.*

explore *(explores exploring explored)*

When you **explore**, you look around a place you have not been to before to see what it is like. *The children explored the garden of their new home.*

expression

Your **expression** is the look on your face that shows how you feel. *You should have seen his expression when he opened the birthday present!*

extinct

If a plant or an animal is **extinct**, there are no more of that kind living on the Earth. *Pterosaurs were flying reptiles that are now extinct.*

extra

Extra means more than usual or more than you need. *We took some extra food for the journey in case Sam decided to come with us.*

extremely

Extremely means very, very. Whales and elephants are **extremely** big creatures.

eye

Your **eyes** are the two parts, on each side of your face that you use for seeing.

Ff

face
Your **face** is the front part of your head, where your eyes, mouth and nose are. *The old man had a very interesting face.*

fact
A **fact** is something that is true. *We told the teacher all the facts.*

factory *(factories)*
A **factory** is a building where people work with machines to make things. *Cars and computers are made in factories.*

fair
1 Something that is **fair** seems good and right. *The teacher was fair and gave everyone a chance to speak.*
2 **Fair** hair and skin are light in colour.
3 A **fair** is a place outside where you can have fun. You can ride on big machines such as roundabouts, and play games to win prizes.

fairy *(fairies)*
A **fairy** is a very small magical person that you can read about in stories. **Fairies** have wings and can fly.

fall *(falls falling fell fallen)*
When somebody or something **falls**, they go down to the ground. *Leaves fall from the trees in autumn. Sally fell off the wall and broke her arm.*

false
If something is **false**, it is not true or real. *Theo is wearing a false nose and moustache.*

family *(families)*
A **family** is usually made up of parents and children. **Families** can also include grandparents, cousins, uncles and aunts.

famous
If somebody or something is **famous**, a lot of people know about them. *Have you ever met anybody famous?*

far *(farther farthest)*
Far means a long way away. *Sam lives farther from school than Phoebe but not as far as Jane.*

farm
A **farm** is a place where people keep animals or grow plants for food. The person who looks after a farm is called a **farmer**.

fast
Something that is **fast** can move quickly. *My mum has a fast car.*

fat
1 *(fatter fattest)* A person or an animal that is **fat** has a large round body.
2 Butter and oil that we use for cooking are also called **fat**. *Fry the vegetables in a little fat.*

father
A **father** is a man who has a child.

fault
If something bad is your **fault**, you made it happen. *It was David's fault I fell over - he pushed me.*

favourite
Your **favourite** is the one that you like best. *What's your favourite colour? Mine is blue.*

fear
Fear is what you feel when you think that something really nasty is going to happen.

feather
Feathers are the light soft things that cover a bird's body. **Feathers** help to keep a bird warm.

feed *(feeds feeding fed)*
If you **feed** a person or an animal, you give them food. *I always feed my dog in the mornings.*

feel *(feels feeling felt)*
1 If you **feel** something, you touch it or it touches you. *Feel how smooth this wood is. Can you feel rain on your face?*
2 If you **feel** ill or happy, that is the way you are. *I feel a bit hungry.*

feet Look at **foot**.

fell Look at **fall**.
Joe fell out of the tree and broke his right leg.

felt Look at **feel**.
I felt sad when my cousins went home to Australia.

female
A **female** is a person or an animal that can have babies. Women and girls are **females**, and men and boys are males.

fence
A **fence** is usually made of wood or wire. **Fences** are put around fields and gardens.

fetch *(fetches fetching fetched)*
If you **fetch** something, you go to get it and bring it back. *Mum asked the waiter to fetch her a clean knife and fork.*

few
Few means not many of something. *There are only a few chocolates left in the box.*

field
A **field** is a piece of land where farmers grow plants for food or keep animals. A **field** can also be a piece of land where you play sports such as football.

fierce
An animal that is **fierce** is frightening and dangerous. *That dog looks fierce!*

fight *(fights fighting fought)*
When people **fight**, they are angry and they are trying to hurt one another.

figure
A **figure** is one of the signs that we use for writing numbers, such as 1, 2, 3 and so on.

fill *(fills filling filled)*
If you **fill** something, you put as much into it as it can hold. *I filled the jug with water.*

film
1 A **film** is a story in moving pictures that you watch on a screen. *Last night there was a really good film on TV.*

2 A **film** is also a roll of plastic that you put inside a camera to take photos.

finally
Finally means at last or at the end. *The climbers finally reached the top of the mountain.*

find *(finds finding found)*
When you **find** something that you were looking for, you see it. *Mark looked everywhere for his glasses and then found them in a drawer.*

fine
1 **Fine** means good. *I felt ill, but I'm fine now.*
2 A **fine** day is sunny and warm.
3 A **fine** is money that you have to pay as a punishment for doing something wrong. *He had to pay a fine for parking his car in a "No Parking" area.*

finger
Your **fingers** are the parts that you can move at the end of your hand. *You have five fingers on each of your hands.*

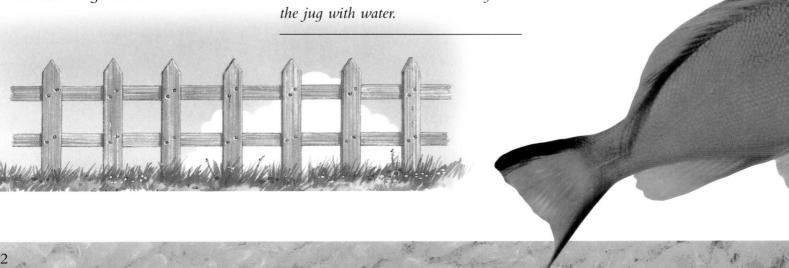

finish (finishes finishing finished)
When you **finish** something, you get to the end of it. *Can I borrow that book when you've finished it?*

fire
Fire is the heat, flames and light that are made by something that is burning.

firefighter
A **firefighter** is a person who puts out fires. **Firefighters** ride in a truck called a fire engine.

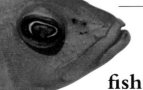

fireworks
Fireworks are paper tubes filled with a special powder. When you light **fireworks**, they send out a shower of bright coloured lights. Some **fireworks** make a loud bang as well.

first
First means at the beginning or before anything else. *January is the first month of the year.*

fish
(fish or fishes)
A **fish** is an animal that lives in water. **Fish** are covered in scales, and they have parts called gills for breathing.

fist
If you close your hand tightly, you make a **fist**.

fit
1 *(fits fitting fitted)* If something **fits**, it is not too big or too small and it is the right shape. *These red shoes don't fit Laura.*
2 *(fitter fittest)* A person who is **fit** is healthy and strong. *My mum goes running every morning to keep fit.*

fix (fixes fixing fixed)
1 If you **fix** things together, you join them.
2 If you **fix** something that was broken, you mend it. *Helen fixed the tap to stop it dripping.*

flag
A **flag** is a piece of cloth with colours and patterns on it. **Flags** fly on poles. Every country has a **flag**.

flame
Flames are the bright moving lights that you see in a fire.

flash (flashes)
A **flash** is a bright light that appears and disappears again very quickly. *Before the thunder there was a flash of lightning.*

flat
1 *(flatter flattest)* If something is **flat**, it is smooth and has no parts that are higher than the rest. The top of a table is **flat**.
2 A **flat** is a set of rooms in a building for living in. **Flats** are usually on one floor. *Do you live in a flat or a house?*

flavour
The **flavour** of food is what it tastes like.

flew Look at fly.
The kite flew high above the trees.

float (floats floating floated)
If something **floats**, it stays on the top of a liquid, or it moves gently in the air. *The balloon floated over the roof. Wood floats on water.*

flood
A **flood** is a lot of water that suddenly covers an area of land that is usually dry. **Floods** sometimes happen after heavy rain or when snow melts.

floor
1 A **floor** is the part of a building that you walk on. *The puppy left mud all over the floor.*
2 A building that has more than one **floor** has rooms on top of other rooms. A block of flats usually has several **floors**.

flour
Flour is a powder made from wheat that we use for baking bread and cakes. It can be white or brown in colour.

flow (flows flowing flowed)
When a liquid such as water **flows**, it moves along. *The river flows into the sea.*

flower

A **flower** is the pretty coloured part of a plant, where the seeds are made.

fly

1 *(flies flying flew flown)* When something **flies**, it moves through the air. Insects, birds and aeroplanes **fly**.
2 *(flies)* A **fly** is a small insect which has wings.

foal

A **foal** is a young horse.

fog

Fog is thick grey cloud near the ground. You cannot see far in **fog**.

fold *(folds folding folded)*

If you **fold** something, you bend one part over another part. *Fold the paper carefully in half.*

follow *(follows following followed)*

If you **follow** somebody or something, you go along behind them. *My little brother follows me everywhere and copies everything I do.*

food

Food is all the things that people and animals eat to stay alive and grow.

foot *(feet)*

Your **foot** is the part at the end of your leg. You stand and walk on your **feet**.

football

Football is a game played by two teams who kick a ball and try to score goals.

forehead

Your **forehead** is the part of your face that is above your eyes and just below your hair.

forest

A **forest** is a large area of land where a lot of trees are growing. *We had a picnic in the forest.*

forget *(forgets forgetting forgot forgotten)*

If you **forget** something, you cannot remember it. *You told me your telephone number, but I've forgotten it.*

forgive *(forgives forgiving forgave forgiven)*

If you **forgive** somebody for doing something bad, you stop being angry with them. *Thomas forgave his sister when she said she was sorry for breaking his train.*

fork

A **fork** is a tool with a long handle and pointed parts called prongs at the end. You use one kind of **fork** to pick up food and put it in your mouth. You use a big **fork** for digging the ground.

forwards

Forwards means in the direction of what is in front of you.

fossil

A **fossil** is what is left of an animal or a plant that lived a long time ago. You can sometimes find **fossils** in rocks.

fought Look at **fight**.
The armies fought a long battle.

found Look at **find**.
Chris found some money in the street.

fox *(foxes)*

A **fox** is a wild animal with red-brown fur and a long thick tail. **Foxes** look a bit like dogs. They live in the countryside and in the towns.

frame

A **frame** is the wooden or metal part that fits around something such as a picture, a photograph or a window.

free

1 If something is **free**, you do not have to pay any money for it. *Children under five travel free on buses in most towns.*
2 If a person or an animal is **free**, there is nothing to stop them going where they want or doing what they like. *Animals in the wild are free.*

freeze *(freezes freezing froze frozen)*

When water **freezes**, it changes into ice. You can **freeze** food to stop it going bad.

fresh

1 Food that is **fresh** is not old or bad. *fresh fish.*
2 **Fresh** water comes from lakes and rivers and is not salty like water from the sea.
3 **Fresh** air is clean and good to breathe.

friend

A **friend** is somebody that you like and who likes you too.

friendly *(friendlier friendliest)*

A person who is **friendly** is kind and helpful.

frighten *(frightens frightening frightened)*

If something **frightens** you, it makes you afraid. *She's frightened of spiders.*

frog

A **frog** is a small animal with strong back legs for jumping. **Frogs** live near water.

front

The **front** of something is the part that you usually see first. Your face is on the **front** of your head. *There is a big oak tree in front of our house.*

frost

Frost is ice-like white powder that covers things outside when the weather is very cold.

frown

When you **frown**, you pull your eyebrows down to show that you are angry or thinking hard.

froze, frozen

Look at **freeze**.
The pond froze last night. We bought a packet of frozen peas.

fruit

Fruit is the part of a plant that has seeds in it. Apples, pineapples, lemons and oranges are all kinds of **fruit**.

fry *(fries frying fried)*

If you **fry** food, you cook it in hot fat. *The sausages were frying in the pan.*

full

If something is **full**, it cannot hold any more. *The car park is full.*

fun

If you are having **fun**, you are happy and enjoying yourself.

funny *(funnier funniest)*

1 Something that is **funny** makes you laugh. *Have you seen that film? It's really funny.*
2 **Funny** can also mean strange. *There's a funny noise coming from next door.*

fur

Fur is the thick hair that covers the body of animals such as cats, dogs and rabbits.

furniture

Beds, chairs, desks and tables are all pieces of **furniture**.

furry

An animal that is **furry** is covered in fur. Hamsters are **furry**.

future

The **future** is the time that has not happened yet. Tomorrow is in the **future**.

Gg

gallop *(gallops galloping galloped)*
When a horse **gallops**, it runs very fast.

game
A **game** is something that you play for fun. **Games** have special rules. Cricket and football are **games**, and so is chess.

gap
A **gap** is an empty space between two things. *Rosie has a gap where her tooth has fallen out.*

garage
1 A **garage** is a building where cars are kept.
2 A **garage** is also a place that sells petrol or mends cars.

garden
A **garden** is a piece of land by a house where people grow flowers and vegetables.

gas *(gases)*
Gas is something that is not solid or liquid and it has no shape. There are many different **gases**. We use one kind of **gas** to cook food and warm our homes. Air is a mixture of other **gases**.

gate
A **gate** is a door in a fence or wall. *Please shut the gate so the dog doesn't get out.*

gave Look at **give**.
Auntie Sue gave me a calculator for my birthday.

geese Look at **goose**.

gentle
A person who is **gentle** is quiet, careful and kind. *Be gentle with the younger children.*

gerbil
A **gerbil** is a small furry animal with long back legs. Some people keep **gerbils** as pets.

ghost
A **ghost** is the shape of a dead person that some people believe they have seen.

giant
A **giant** is a very big person in stories.

gift
A **gift** is a present.

giggle *(giggles giggling giggled)*
If you **giggle**, you laugh in a high voice.
The children all giggled when the clown fell over.

giraffe
A **giraffe** is a wild animal with a very long neck and long legs. **Giraffes** live in Africa.

girl
A **girl** is a female child. **Girls** grow up to be women.

give *(gives giving gave given)*
If you **give** something to somebody, you let them have it. *Ben didn't want his cake so he gave it to me.*

glad
If you are **glad** about something, you are happy about it. *I'm glad you like your present.*

glass
1 Glass is a hard material that you can see through. Windows are made of **glass**.
2 *(glasses)* A **glass** is something you drink from.

glasses
Some people wear **glasses** over their eyes to help them see better. **Glasses** are made of two pieces of special glass joined together in a frame.

glove
A **glove** has parts that cover each finger and thumb. People wear **gloves** to keep their hands warm or to protect them.

glue
Glue is a thick liquid that you use for sticking things together.

goal
1 A **goal** is the net between two posts that players have to kick or hit a ball into in games such as football.
2 A **goal** is also a point that you score when you hit or kick a ball into the goal in a game.

goat

A **goat** is an animal with short rough hair. Some **goats** have horns. **Goats** are sometimes kept on farms for their milk.

gold

Gold is a shiny yellow metal that is used to make things such as rings, necklaces and coins. **Gold** costs a lot of money.

good *(better best)*

1 If something is **good**, you like and enjoy it. *This is a good book.*
2 If you are **good** at something, you do it well. *My sister is really good at tennis.*
3 If a person or an animal is **good**, they do what they are told. *Mum asked us to be good while she was out.*
4 A person who is **good** is kind and helpful.

goose *(geese)*

A **goose** is a large bird with a long neck. **Geese** can swim and they live near water.

grab *(grabs grabbing grabbed)*

If you **grab** something, you take hold of it suddenly. *She grabbed the little boy's hand as he was about to step into the road.*

grandfather

Your **grandfather** is the father of your mother or father.

grandmother

Your **grandmother** is the mother of your father or of your mother.

grape

A **grape** is a small round green or purple fruit. **Grapes** grow in bunches on a bush called a grapevine.

grapefruit

A **grapefruit** is a round fruit like a big orange but with a yellow skin.

grass

Grass is a plant with thin green leaves. **Grass** grows in fields and gardens. Cows and horses and other animals eat **grass**.

great

1 Great means very good or very important. *It was a great party. She is a great actor.*
2 Great can also mean very big. *She gave me a great big kiss!*

grew Look at **grow**.

The little puppy soon grew into a huge dog.

ground

The **ground** is what we walk on when we are outside.

group

A **group** is a number of things that are in one place. *There is a group of tall trees in the park. I'll meet you there.*

grow *(grows growing grew grown)*

When somebody or something **grows**, they become bigger or taller. *The seed we planted will grow into a tall tree.*

grownup

A **grownup** is a person who is not a child any more.

guard *(guards guarding guarded)*

To **guard** means to watch somebody or something to make sure that nothing bad happens to them. *A big dog guards the chocolate factory at night.*

guess *(guesses guessing guessed)*

When you **guess**, you try to think of an answer to something without knowing if the answer is right. *Can you guess what I've bought Paul for his birthday?*

guinea-pig

A **guinea-pig** is a small furry animal with no tail. Some people keep **guinea-pigs** as pets.

guitar

A **guitar** is a musical instrument with strings that you play with your fingers. *I am learning to play the guitar.*

gym

A **gym** is a room where you can play games or do exercises to keep your body fit and strong.

Hh

habit
A **habit** is something you do so often that you do not think about it. *Brushing your teeth after meals is a good habit.*

hair
Hair is what grows on your head. *Lily has long red hair.*

half *(halves)*
A **half** is one of two parts of something that are the same size. Two **halves** make a whole.

hall
1 A **hall** is a room in a house or flat that has doors leading to the other rooms.
2 A **hall** is also a very big room. *All the children in our school meet in the hall every morning for assembly.*

hamburger
A **hamburger** is a flat round kind of food made from tiny pieces of meat. We eat **hamburgers** in bread rolls.

hammer
A **hammer** is a heavy tool that people use to hit nails into things.

hamster
A **hamster** is a small furry animal that can store food in its cheeks. Some people keep **hamsters** as pets.

hand
Your **hands** are at the end of your arms. A **hand** has four fingers and a thumb. We use our **hands** to pick things up and to hold them.

handle
A **handle** is part of something that you use for holding or moving it with your hand. Things such as cups, doors and knives have **handles**.

hang *(hangs hanging hung)*
When you **hang** something somewhere, you fix the top of it to something above it. *Emily hung her coat up on the hook.*

happy *(happier happiest)*
When you are **happy**, you feel good about something and you laugh or smile a lot.

hard
1 If something is **hard**, you cannot shape or break it easily with your hands. *Nutshells are hard but stones are harder.*
2 If something is **hard** to do, it is difficult. *These sums are quite hard. Can you help me with them?*

hat
A **hat** is something you wear on your head to keep it warm or dry.

hatch *(hatches hatching hatched)*
A baby bird **hatches** when it breaks out of an egg.

hate *(hates hating hated)*
If you **hate** somebody or something, you do not like them at all.

haunted
If people say that a place is **haunted**, they mean that a ghost is supposed to live there. *I read a story about a haunted house.*

hay
Hay is dry grass that is used to feed animals such as horses and cattle in winter.

head
1 Your **head** is the part of your body above your neck. Your face and ears are part of your **head**.
2 A **head** is also the person in charge. *We have a new head teacher at our school.*

headache
If you have a **headache**, your head hurts.

heal *(heals healing healed)*
When a cut **heals**, it gets better. *He cut his finger but it soon healed.*

health
Your **health** is how well your body is. *Fresh fruit and vegetables are good for your health.*

healthy *(healthier healthiest)*
If you are **healthy**, you feel really well. *a healthy child.*

hear (hears hearing heard)
When you **hear** something, you take in sounds through your ears. *Did you hear the thunder?*

heart
Your **heart** is inside your chest. It sends blood around your body. You can feel the beat of your **heart** when you run.

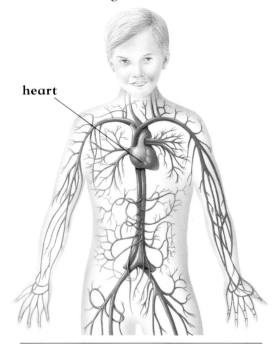

heart

heat
1 Heat is what makes things warm. *I can feel the heat of the sun.*
2 (heats heating heated) If you **heat** something, you make it warm. *Dad heated up the soup in a pan.*

heavy (heavier heaviest)
Something that is **heavy** is difficult to lift. *The large box is heavier than the suitcase.*

heel
Your **heel** is the round part at the back of your foot.

height
The **height** of something is how tall or high it is.

held Look at **hold**.
Hannah held the kitten.

helicopter
A **helicopter** is an aircraft without wings. **Helicopters** have long blades on the top that turn around very fast.

helmet
A **helmet** is a hard metal or plastic hat that protects your head. *I wear my cycle helmet when I go on bike rides.*

help (helps helping helped)
If you **help** somebody, you do something useful for them. *Ella helped her grandma carry her shopping.*

hen
Hens are chickens that lay eggs.

hide (hides hiding hid hidden)
If you **hide** something, you put it where nobody can see it. *Where have you hidden my birthday present?*

high
Something that is **high** goes up a long way. *We couldn't see over the fence because it was too high.*

hill
A **hill** is a piece of land that is higher than the land around it.

hippopotamus (hippopotamuses)
A **hippopotamus** is a large wild animal with short legs and a big mouth. **Hippopotamuses** live near lakes and rivers in Africa and like to take mud baths. They are often called hippos for short.

hit (hits hitting hit)
If you **hit** something, you touch it very hard. *Ewen hit the ball and it hit me on the head.*

hive
A **hive** is a box for keeping bees in. Bees make honey in **hives**. *My granddad has a beehive in his back garden.*

hobby (hobbies)
A **hobby** is something that people like doing when they are not working. *My brother's hobbies are collecting coins and fishing.*

hold (holds holding held)
1 When you **hold** something, you have it in your hand. *Jemma held her little sister's hand.*
2 To **hold** also means to have space inside for something. *How much milk does the carton hold?*

hole
A **hole** is a gap or empty space in something. *The children dug holes in the sand.*

holiday
A **holiday** is a time when you do not work or go to school.

hollow
Something that is **hollow** is empty inside.

home

Your **home** is where you live.

honey

Honey is a sweet sticky liquid that bees make. *I like honey on my bread for breakfast.*

hoof *(hooves)*

A **hoof** is the hard part of a horse's foot. Cattle, sheep and deer also have **hooves**.

hop *(hops hopping hopped)*

1 When you **hop**, you jump on one foot.
2 When an animal **hops** it moves along in small jumps.

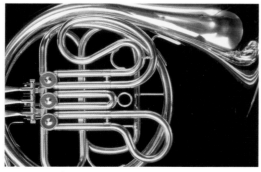

hope *(hopes hoping hoped)*

If you **hope** that something will happen, you want it to happen very much and you believe that it will. *My sister is hoping to get a new bike for her birthday.*

horn

1 A **horn** is one of the hard pointed things that grow out of the head of some animals. Cows and goats have **horns**.
2 A **horn** is also a musical instrument that you play by blowing into it.

horrible

If something is **horrible**, it is nasty or frightening. *This food tastes really horrible.*

horse

A **horse** is a large animal with hooves. Some people like to ride **horses**.

hospital

A **hospital** is a large building where doctors and nurses look after people who are ill or hurt.

hot *(hotter hottest)*

Something that is **hot** can burn you if you touch it. *Don't touch the oven - it's very hot.*

hotel

A **hotel** is a building with lots of bedrooms where people can stay when they are away from home.

hour

An **hour** has sixty minutes. There are twenty-four **hours** in a day.

house

A **house** is a building that people live in.

hug *(hugs hugging hugged)*

If you **hug** somebody, you put your arms around them and hold them tight. *Tom hugged his aunt when she left.*

huge

Something that is **huge** is very big. *That's a huge plate of chips!*

human

A **human** is a man, woman or child.

hump

A **hump** is a big round lump on the back of a camel.

hung Look at **hang**.
I hung my coat on the hook.

hungry *(hungrier hungriest)*

When you are **hungry**, you want something to eat.

hunt *(hunts hunting hunted)*

1 When animals **hunt**, they chase other animals to catch them and eat them.
2 If you **hunt** for something, you look carefully for it. *We hunted everywhere for Mum's necklace.*

hurry *(hurries hurrying hurried)*

When you **hurry**, you do something very quickly. *Unless you hurry you'll miss the bus.*

hurt *(hurts hurting hurt)*

If a part of your body **hurts**, you feel pain there. *My finger hurt when I hit it with a hammer.*

husband

A woman's **husband** is the man that she is married to.

hut

A **hut** is a very small simple house. Many **huts** are made of wood or grass.

hutch

A **hutch** is a cage for a pet rabbit or guinea pig.

Ii

ice
Ice is water that is frozen so that it is hard. *The pond is covered with a layer of ice.*

iceberg
An **iceberg** is a huge block of ice that floats in the sea.

ice-cream
Ice-cream is a soft sweet frozen food.

ice-skating
When you go **ice-skating** you slide along the ice in special boots called ice-skates that have a thin piece of metal on the bottom.

icicle
An **icicle** is a long, pointed piece of ice that hangs down.

icing
Icing is a smooth, sweet paste made of sugar that you sometimes spread over cakes.

idea
An **idea** is something you have thought of. *I've got a good idea for a birthday present.*

igloo
An **igloo** is a round house made of blocks of snow and ice.

iguana
An **iguana** is a large lizard that lives in trees in hot countries.

ill
If you are **ill** you are not well. *Jasmine is too ill to go to school today.*

illness
An **illness** is something that makes you feel ill. *Jill is recovering from her illness.*

imagine *(imagines imagining imagined)*
If you **imagine** something, you have a picture of it in your mind. *Can you imagine what the world was like when dinosaurs were alive?*

imitate *(imitates imitating imitated)*
If you **imitate** somebody, you try to copy or do the same as them. *Sam made us laugh when he tried to imitate a dog barking.*

immediately
When you do something **immediately**, you do it now, without waiting. *Go to your room immediately!*

important
1 Something that is **important** matters a lot. *It's important to eat well if you want to stay healthy.*

2 An **important** person is a person who is powerful or special in some way.

impossible
If something is **impossible** it cannot be done. *It's impossible for a person to walk on water.*

information
Information is the facts that tell you about something. *We need some information about the times of trains to Bristol.*

initial
An **initial** is the first letter of a name or word. *Jane Adam's initials are J.A.*

injection
If a doctor or a nurse gives you an **injection**, they put medicine into your body by pushing a special needle into your skin.

injure
If you **injure** yourself, you hurt a part of your body. *Jim injured his arm when he fell off his bike.*

ink
Ink is a coloured liquid that we use for writing and printing.

insect

An **insect** is a small creature with six legs. Some **insects** have wings and can fly. Ants, bees, butterflies and flies are different kinds of **insects**, but spiders are not.

instead

Instead means in the place of somebody or something. *We couldn't go to the beach because it was raining, so we watched a film instead.*

instructions

Instructions are words or pictures that tell you how to do something. *The video recorder is quite easy to use if you follow the instructions properly.*

instrument

1 An **instrument** is a tool that helps you to do something. *A microscope is an instrument for looking at tiny objects.*
2 A musical **instrument** is something that you play to make music. Drums, pianos, trumpets and violins are types of musical **instruments**.

interesting

If something is **interesting**, you like it and you want to find out more about it. *That was a very interesting programme.*

interfere *(interferes interfering interfered)*

If you **interfere**, you try to do something for somebody when they do not want your help. *My little sister keeps interfering when I'm playing my computer game.*

interrupt *(interrupts interrupting interrupted)*

If you **interrupt** somebody, you stop them doing or saying something for a moment. *Kurt interrupted me when I was talking on the phone.*

interview

An **interview** is when you meet somebody to answer questions about yourself. *She watched an interview about her favourite singer.*

invent *(invents inventing invented)*

If you **invent** something, you are the first person to think of it or to make it. *I wonder who invented the first computer?*

invention

An **invention** is something new that somebody invents. *Televisions and computers are great inventions.*

inventor

An **inventor** is a person who invents things.

invisible

If something is **invisible**, it cannot be seen. Air is **invisible**. *The magician did a trick and made the rabbit invisible.*

invite *(invites inviting invited)*

If you **invite** somebody, you ask them to visit you or to do something with you. *Sophie invited her friends to a party. She wrote out invitations and then posted them to everybody.*

iron

1 Iron is a strong heavy metal.
2 An **iron** is a kind of tool with a flat metal bottom. We make an **iron** hot and use it to make clothes smooth and flat.

island

An **island** is a piece of land with water all around it.

itch *(itches itching itched)*

When a part of your body **itches**, you want to scratch it.

ivy

Ivy is a plant with shiny leaves that climbs up walls and trees. *Our old garden wall is covered in ivy.*

Jj

jacket
A **jacket** is a short coat. *Matt is wearing a blue denim jacket.*

jail
A **jail** is a place where some people have to stay when they have done something that is against the law.

jam
1 **Jam** is a sweet food made by cooking fruit and sugar together for a long time.
2 A traffic **jam** is a lot of cars so close together that they cannot move. *We were late because we got stuck in a traffic jam.*
3 *(jams jamming jammed)* If something **jams**, it becomes difficult to move. *The door won't open because it's jammed.*

jar
A **jar** is a wide glass container. You buy jam in a **jar**.

jealous
If you are **jealous** of somebody, you feel angry or unhappy because they have something that you would like to have.

jeans
Jeans are trousers made from strong cotton cloth called denim.

jelly *(jellies)*
Jelly is a sweet food that you can see through. **Jelly** shakes when you move it.

jet
A **jet** is an aeroplane that can fly very fast.

jewel
A **jewel** is a beautiful stone such as a diamond or an emerald. **Jewels** are worth a lot of money and they are used to make things such as rings and necklaces.

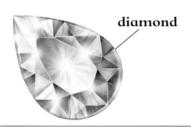

diamond

job
1 A **job** is the work that somebody does to earn money.
2 A **job** is also something that has to be done. *Why is it always my job to feed the cat?*

join *(joins joining joined)*
1 If you **join** things, you put or fix them together. *She joined the two pieces of wood with glue.*
2 If you **join** something such as a club, you become part of it.

joke
A **joke** is a kind of short story that makes people laugh.

journey
When you go on a **journey**, you travel from one place to another.

juice
Juice is the liquid that comes out of fruit when you squeeze it.

jump *(jumps jumping jumped)*
When you **jump**, you push yourself up into the air with your feet off the ground.

jumper
A **jumper** is something that you wear to keep you warm. It covers your arms and the top part of your body. **Jumpers** are often made of wool.

jungle
A **jungle** is a thick forest in a hot country where it rains a lot. A lot of different animals live in the **jungles** of the world.

Kk

kangaroo
A **kangaroo** is a wild animal with strong back legs that it uses for jumping. **Kangaroos** live in Australia.

keep
(keeps keeping kept)
1 If you **keep** something, you have it and you do not give it to anybody else. *My best friend gave me this photo and I'm going to keep it for ever.*
2 If you **keep** something in a place, that is where you always put it. *Simon keeps his toy cars in a box under the bed.*
3 If you **keep** doing something, you do it again and again. *Why do you keep making that noise?*
4 Keep can also mean to stay the same way. *Please keep quiet while I'm talking.*

kettle
A **kettle** is a thing that you use for making water hot. A **kettle** has a lid and a pointed part called a spout for pouring.

key
1 A **key** is a piece of metal that you use to open or close a lock.
2 The **keys** of a piano or computer are the parts that you press with your fingers.

kick
(kicks kicking kicked)
If you **kick** something, you hit it with your foot. *Sam kicked the ball into the goal.*

kill
(kills killing killed)
To **kill** is to end the life of somebody or something.
The fox killed a chicken.

kind
1 If you are **kind**, you are nice to people and try to help them. *It was kind of you to do the shopping.*
2 Kind also means a group of things that are the same in some way. *Apples, bananas and plums are all kinds of fruit.*

king
Some countries have a ruler who is a man called a **king**. The wife of a **king** is called a queen.

kingdom
A **kingdom** is a country where a king or queen rules.

kiss
(kisses kissing kissed)
When you **kiss** somebody, you touch them with your lips to show that you like or love them. *Billy always kisses his dad before he goes to bed.*

kit
A **kit** is a set of tools or equipment that you need to do something. *I got a puppet-making kit for my birthday.*

kitchen
A **kitchen** is a room where people cook food.

kite
A **kite** is a toy that you can fly on windy days by holding the end of a long string.

kitten
A **kitten** is a very young cat.

knee
Your **knee** is the part in the middle of your leg where it bends.

kneel
(kneels kneeling knelt)
When you **kneel**, you go down on your knees.

knife
(knives)
A **knife** is a tool with a sharp edge called a blade for cutting.

knight
A **knight** was a soldier who lived a long time ago. **Knights** rode into battle on horses, and many **knights** wore armour.

knit
(knits knitting knitted)
When people **knit**, they use wool and needles to make clothes such as jumpers.

knock
(knocks knocking knocked)
When you **knock** something, you hit it. *Who's knocking at the door?*

knot
You make a **knot** when you twist and tie pieces of string or ribbon. *Can you untie this knot in my shoelace?*

koala
A **koala** is a grey furry animal that looks like a small bear. **Koalas** live in trees in Australia.

L1

ladder
A **ladder** is a set of steps that you climb up to reach high places. You can carry **ladders** from one place to another.

ladybird
A **ladybird** is a small beetle. It has a red or yellow body with black spots. **Ladybirds** can fly.

lain
Look at **lie**.
She must have lain down and fallen fast asleep.

lake
A **lake** is a lot of water with land all around it.

lamb
A **lamb** is a young sheep.
The lambs played in the field.

lamp
A **lamp** is something that gives light where you need it. Most **lamps** use electricity. *Freddie has a lamp on his desk to help him see what he is doing.*

land
1 **Land** is any part of the Earth that is not covered in water.
2 *(lands landing landed)* When an aeroplane or bird **lands**, it stops flying and comes down on to the ground. *The plane has just landed.*

language
A **language** is all the words that the people of one country use to speak or write to each other. *People in France speak a language that is called French.*

lap
Your **lap** is the top part of your legs when you are sitting down. *Christina is sitting on her mum's lap.*

large
Something that is **large** is big. *An elephant is a very large animal.*

last
1 If somebody or something is **last**, they are at the end or they come after all the others. *Z is the last letter of the alphabet.*
2 **Last** also means before this one. *Last week we were at school, but this week is a holiday.*
3 *(lasts lasting lasted)* To **last** means to go on for a certain amount of time. *The film lasted nearly two-and-a-half hours.*

late
If you are **late**, you get to a place after the usual time or after the time that you were supposed to. *Lucy was late for school this morning because she woke up late.*

laugh *(laughs laughing laughed)*
When people **laugh**, they make sounds to show that they think something is funny.

law
Laws are the rules made by a country. They tell people what they can and cannot do. *Stealing other people's money is against the law.*

lawn
A **lawn** is a part of a park or garden that is covered in grass. You cut a **lawn** with a machine called a lawnmower.

lay *(lays laying laid)*
1 When you **lay** something somewhere, you put it down carefully. *Liam laid the box of eggs on the table.*
2 When you **lay** a table, you put things such as knives and forks on it, ready for a meal.
3 When a bird **lays** an egg, the egg comes out of the bird's body. *Our duck laid five eggs in her nest this morning.*
4 Look at **lie**.
Jenny lay on her bed and read her favourite book.

layer

A **layer** is a flat piece of something that lies on or under something else. *The cake had a layer of icing on top and two layers of jam in the middle.*

lazy *(lazier laziest)*

A person who is **lazy** does not want to work or does not want to do very much at all. *Come on you lazy girl - time to get up!*

lead

1 *(leads leading led)* When you **lead** somebody to a place, you go in front to show them where it is. *The woman at the cinema led us to our seats.*
2 *(leads leading led)* If a road or path **leads** to a place, it goes there. *This path leads to the beach.*
3 A **lead** is a rope, chain or long piece of leather that you fix to a dog's collar so that you can control the dog when you take it for walks.

lead

Lead is a heavy grey metal that is quite soft.

leader

A **leader** is a person who is in charge of other people.

leaf *(leaves)*

A **leaf** is one of the flat thin parts that grow on the stem of a plant. Most **leaves** are green. In autumn, **leaves** change colour and fall off some trees.

lean *(leans leaning leant or leaned)*

To **lean** means to bend one way or to rest against something. *Josh leant his bike against the wall.*

learn *(learns learning learnt or learned)*

When you **learn**, you find out about something or how to do something. *My little brother is learning to read.*

leather

Leather is a material made from the skin of animals. A lot of shoes are made of **leather**.

leave *(leaves leaving left)*

1 When you **leave**, you go away from a place.
2 If you **leave** something somewhere, you do not take it with you. *I left my bike at home and walked to school.*

leaves Look at **leaf**.

The leaves fall off the trees in autumn.

led Look at **lead**.

Hassan led me to his room.

left

1 You are reading the words on this page from the **left** to the right. **Left** is the opposite of right.
2 Look at **leave**.

He left his bag on the bus.

leg

1 **Legs** are the long parts of your body that you use for walking on. People have two **legs**, and cows and dogs have four **legs**.
2 The **legs** of a chair or table are the parts that it stands on.

lemon

A **lemon** is a yellow fruit with a thick skin that tastes very sour.

length

The **length** of something is how long it is.

lesson

A **lesson** is a time when somebody is teaching you something. *Lina has ballet lessons twice a week.*

letter

1 A **letter** is one of the signs that we use for writing words, such as A, B and C. **Letters** make up the alphabet.
2 A **letter** is also a message that you write on paper and send to somebody.

lettuce

A **lettuce** is a vegetable with large green leaves that we eat raw in salads.

library *(libraries)*

A **library** is a place where books are kept for people to borrow and read at home. A lot of **libraries** also have computers where you can find information.

lick *(licks licking licked)*

When you **lick** something, you touch it with your tongue to taste it or to make it wet.

lid

A **lid** is the top part that covers a container such as a jar or box. *Put the lid back on the biscuit tin when you've finished with it.*

lie

1 A **lie** is something you say that you know is not true. *She said she was going straight home but it was a lie. She went to her best friend's house instead.*

2 *(lies lying lay lain)* When you **lie** somewhere, you put your body down flat so that you are not sitting or standing. *Lie down and go to sleep.*

life *(lives)*

Your **life** is the time when you are living on the earth.

lift

1 *(lifts lifting lifted)* When you **lift** something, you pick it up. *This box is too heavy for me to lift by myself.*

2 A **lift** is a kind of box that travels up and down inside tall buildings to carry people and things to different floors.

light

1 **Light** comes from the Sun and from lamps. Without **light** it would be dark and we would not be able to see anything.

2 Something that is **light** is easy to lift. *Feathers are light.*

3 **Light** colours are pale. *Tom's T-shirt is light green.*

4 *(lights lighting lit)* When you **light** something, you start it burning. *We lit the candles on the cake.*

lighthouse

A **lighthouse** is a tower near the sea with a bright light on top. **Lighthouses** show ships where there are dangerous rocks.

lightning

Lightning is the flash of light that you see in the sky when there is a thunderstorm.

like

1 *(likes liking liked)* If you **like** somebody or something, they make you happy. *Billy likes dancing.*

2 If something is **like** something else, it is the same in some way. *Jodie looks like her sister.*

likely

If something is **likely**, it will probably happen. *It's likely to rain this evening.*

line

1 A **line** is a long thin mark. *It's easier to draw a straight line if you use a ruler.*

2 A **line** is also a row of people or things. *Stand in a line.*

lion

A **lion** is a large wild animal of the cat family. **Lions** live in Africa. A female **lion** is a lioness.

lip

Your **lips** are the two soft pink edges of your mouth.

liquid

A **liquid** is anything wet that you can pour. Water, oil and milk are all **liquids**.

list

A **list** is a group of things that you write down one after the other. *Make a list of all the people that you would like to invite to your birthday party.*

listen *(listens listening listened)*

When you **listen**, you are trying carefully to hear something. *If you listen, you can hear the sound of the sea in the distance.*

lit Look at **light**.
It was cold so Cleo lit the fire.

litter

1 **Litter** is rubbish such as bits of paper that people have left lying around.

2 A **litter** is all the baby animals that a mother has at one time. *The pig has had a litter of piglets.*

little

1 Something that is **little** is small. *A mouse is a little animal.*

2 A **little** means not very much. *The cat only drank a little milk.*

live *(lives living lived)*

1 To **live** means to be alive and growing. *People need air, food and water to live.*

2 If you **live** somewhere, that is where your home is. *We live near the park.*

lives Look at **life**.
We have been here all our lives.

loaf (loaves)

A **loaf** is a large piece of bread that can be cut into slices.

lock

1 A **lock** is something that you need a key to open. You use **locks** to keep things like doors, windows and drawers shut.
2 (locks locking locked) If you **lock** something, you keep it closed with a key. *Did you remember to lock the front door?*

log

A **log** is a round piece of wood that has been cut from a tree. People sometimes burn **logs** to make heat.

lonely (lonelier loneliest)

If somebody is **lonely**, they are unhappy because they are all alone.

long

1 Something that is **long** measures a lot from one end to the other. *Giraffes are animals with very long necks.*
2 If something is **long**, it takes a lot of time. *We watched a very long, boring film.*

look (looks looking looked)

1 If you look at something, you turn your eyes towards it to see it. *Look at that huge bird in the tree.*
2 If you look for something, you try to find it. *Can you help me look for my book?*

loose

If something is **loose**, it is not held firmly in place. *Jamie's front tooth is very loose - it will probably fall out soon.*

lorry (lorries)

A **lorry** is a big machine for carrying heavy things by road.

lose (loses losing lost)

1 If you **lose** something, you do not have it any more and you cannot find it. *Larry has lost one of his shoes.*
2 If you **lose** a game, you do not win it. *Our team lost the match by one goal.*

lost

If you are **lost**, you cannot find your way home. *We took the wrong path and got lost in the forest.*

lottery (lotteries)

A **lottery** is a kind of game in which you can win prizes. You pick numbers or buy tickets with numbers on them. If your numbers are chosen, you win.

loud

Something that is **loud** is easy to hear because it makes a lot of noise. *The fireworks exploded with a loud bang.*

love (loves loving loved)

If you **love** somebody or something, you like them very very much.

lovely (lovelier loveliest)

If something is **lovely**, it is beautiful or very nice. *These flowers smell lovely.*

low

Something that is **low** is near the ground. *There's a low wall around the park.*

lower (lowers lowering lowered)

If you **lower** something you move it down. *We watched the bulldozer lowering the logs.*

lucky (luckier luckiest)

If you are **lucky**, nice things happen to you that you did not expect to happen.

luggage

Luggage is all the bags and suitcases that you take with you when you go on holiday.

lump

A **lump** is a solid piece of something, sometimes with a round shape. *Ellie is making a model from some lumps of clay.*

lunch (lunches)

Lunch is a meal that people eat in the middle of the day.

lung

Your **lungs** are the two parts inside your chest that you use for breathing. They fill with air when you breathe in and empty again when you breathe out.

Mm

machine
A **machine** is a thing with moving parts that does a job. Video recorders, computers and aeroplanes are all **machines**.

magazine
A **magazine** is a kind of thin book with pictures and stories that you can buy each week or each month.

magic
Magic is a way of making strange or impossible things seem to happen.

magician
A **magician** is a person who seems to make strange or impossible things happen.

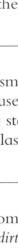

magnet
A **magnet** is a piece of metal that can make other metal things move towards it and stick to it.

magnifying glass
A **magnifying glass** is a special piece of glass. When you look through it, it makes things seem bigger than they really are.

main
Main means the most important. *The village shop is on the main road.*

male
A **male** is a person or an animal that can be a father. Boys and men are **males**, and girls and women are females.

mammal
A **mammal** is an animal that drinks milk from its mother's body when it is young. Dogs, horses, whales and people are different kinds of **mammals**.

man *(men)*
A **man** is a grown-up male.

map
A **map** is a drawing that shows what a place looks like from above. **Maps** show you where different towns are as well as roads, rivers and mountains. People use **maps** to help them find their way about.

marble
1 **Marble** is a kind of smooth hard stone. **Marble** is used in building or for making statues.
2 **Marbles** are small glass balls used in games.

mark
A **mark** is a spot on something that spoils it. *There are dirty marks on your white shirt.*

marry *(marries marrying married)*
When a man and woman **marry**, they become husband and wife.

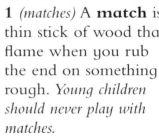

mask
A **mask** is something that you can wear over your face to hide or protect it. Actors in plays sometimes wear **masks**. *We saw people wearing silver masks when we were in Italy.*

match
1 *(matches)* A **match** is a small thin stick of wood that makes a flame when you rub the end on something rough. *Young children should never play with matches.*
2 *(matches)* A **match** is also a game between two teams or players, such as football or cricket or tennis.
3 *(matches matching matched)* If two things **match**, they are the same in some way. *Jenna's top matches her trousers.*

material
1 **Material** is anything that we use to make things with. Wood, glass and paper are all **materials**.
2 **Material** is also cloth that we make clothes from. *Mum bought some material to make me a dress.*

matter *(matters mattering mattered)*
If something **matters**, it is important. *It doesn't matter if we're a bit late.*

mattress *(mattresses)*
A **mattress** is the soft thick part of a bed that you lie on.

meal
A **meal** is all the food that you eat at one time. Breakfast, lunch and dinner are **meals**.

mean
1 *(means meaning meant)* If you tell somebody what something **means**, you try to explain it. *That sign means that you can't park in this street.*
2 *(means meaning meant)* If you **mean** to do something, you plan to do it. *I meant to phone you last night, but I forgot.*
3 A person who is **mean** does not like spending money or giving things to people.

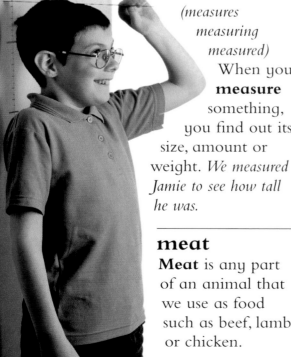

measure *(measures measuring measured)*
When you **measure** something, you find out its size, amount or weight. *We measured Jamie to see how tall he was.*

meat
Meat is any part of an animal that we use as food such as beef, lamb or chicken.

medal
A **medal** is a round piece of metal with writing or a picture on it. **Medals** are given to people who win in sports or who have done something brave.

medicine
Medicine is a pill or liquid that a doctor gives you when you are ill to make you better.

medium
Medium means not big or small, but in between. *a medium-sized T-shirt.*

meet *(meets meeting met)*
When you **meet** somebody, you come together in the same place at the same time. *We agreed to meet after school outside the library in town.*

melt *(melts melting melted)*
When something **melts**, it changes into a liquid as it becomes warmer. *My ice-cream melted in the sun.*

memory
Memory is being able to remember things. *Mary has a good memory - she can remember all her friends' telephone numbers.*

men Look at **man**.
Two men got out of the car.

mend *(mend mending mended)*
When you **mend** something that is broken, you make it useful again. *Luke is trying to mend his bike.*

mess
A **mess** is when things are untidy or dirty. *Please tidy up the mess in your room.*

message
A **message** is words that you send to somebody when you cannot speak to them yourself. *She was out when I phoned but I left a message with her sister.*

met Look at **meet**.
They met at midnight.

metal
Metal is a hard material that melts when it is very hot. Gold, lead and iron are all **metals**.

mice Look at **mouse**.
Our cat likes catching mice.

microscope
A **microscope** is an instrument that makes tiny things look much bigger than they really are.

microwave
A **microwave** is a kind of oven that cooks food very quickly.

midday
Midday is twelve o'clock in the middle of the day.

middle
The **middle** of something is the part that is farthest away from the outsides.

midnight
Midnight is twelve o'clock at night. *We arrived home at midnight.*

milk

Milk is a white liquid that female mammals make in their bodies to feed their babies. People drink the **milk** that comes from cows.

mind

1 Your **mind** is what makes you think, learn, feel and remember.
2 *(minds minding minded)* If you do not **mind** something, it does not worry or upset you. *I don't mind if you borrow my things - as long as you bring them back when you've finished with them.*
3 Mind also means to be careful. *Mind that glass door!*

minus

We use **minus** to talk about taking one number away from another number. We often write **minus** as −. *Seven minus two is five (7−2=5).*

minute

A **minute** is an amount of time. There are sixty seconds in a **minute** and there are sixty **minutes** in an hour.

mirror

A **mirror** is a piece of special glass that you look into to see yourself.

miss *(misses missing missed)*

1 If you **miss** something that you were trying to hit or catch, you do not hit or catch it. *We were late so we missed the train.*
2 If you **miss** somebody, you are unhappy because they are not with you. *I missed my cousins when they went to Africa.*
3 If something is **missing**, it is not there. *Joe's two front teeth are missing because they have fallen out.*

mistake

If you make a **mistake**, you do something wrong, but not on purpose. *Rosie's sums were full of mistakes so she had to do them again.*

mix *(mixes mixing mixed)*

When you **mix** different things, you stir or put them together in some way so that they make something new. *If you mix blue and yellow paint, you get green.*

mixture

A **mixture** is different things that you stir or put together to make something new. *We added melted chocolate to the cake mixture and stirred it.*

model

1 A **model** is a small copy of something. *Peter has just made a model aeroplane.*

2 A **model** is a person who wears new clothes so that other people can see what they look like before they buy them.

moment

A **moment** is a very short time. *Wait here - I'll be back in a moment.*

money

Money is the coins and pieces of paper that we use to buy things.

monkey

A **monkey** is a furry wild animal with long arms and legs and a long tail that it uses to swing through trees. **Monkeys** live in hot countries.

monster

A **monster** is a large fierce animal in stories. *The hydra was a monster in ancient Greek stories which had nine snake heads.*

month

A **month** is a part of a year. There are twelve **months** in a year.

moon

The **Moon** is a planet that travels around the earth once every four weeks. You can often see the **Moon** in the sky at night.

morning

The **morning** is the beginning part of the day. The **morning** ends at twelve o'clock.

moth

A **moth** is an insect with large wings that looks like a butterfly. **Moths** fly at night.

mother

A **mother** is a woman who has a child.

motorbike

A **motorbike** is a kind of heavy bicycle with an engine.

motorway

A **motorway** is a very wide road where traffic can travel fast.

mountain

A **mountain** is a very high hill. *The mountains are covered in snow.*

mouse

A **mouse** is a small furry animal that has a long thin tail and sharp teeth.

mouth

Your **mouth** is the part of your face that you use for eating and speaking. Your teeth and tongue are inside your **mouth**.

move *(moves moving moved)*

If you **move**, you go from one place to another.

mud

Mud is wet sticky earth. *Take off your boots - they are covered in mud.*

mug

A **mug** is a big cup with straight sides and a handle. You drink things like tea and coffee from **mugs**.

multiply *(multiplies multiplying multiplied)*

When you **multiply**, you add a number to itself several times. *Three multiplied by two is six (3x2=6). It is the same as three plus three.*

$$3 \times 2 = 6$$

muscle

Your **muscles** are parts of your body under your skin that get tight and loose and help you to move around.

museum

A **museum** is a building where you can go to see a lot of interesting things. *We saw the bones of a huge dinosaur in the museum.*

mushroom

A **mushroom** is a plant without leaves that is shaped a bit like an umbrella. You can eat some kinds of **mushroom**.

music

Music is the sounds made by people singing or playing musical instruments such as violins, guitars or pianos.

musical instrument

A **musical instrument** is something that you play to make music. Recorders and trumpets are **musical instuments**.

mystery *(mysteries)*

A **mystery** is something strange that has happened that you cannot understand or explain.

Nn

nail

1 Your **nails** are the hard parts at the end of your fingers and toes.

2 A **nail** is also a short piece of metal with a pointed end and flat top. You hit **nails** with a hammer to fix one thing to another.

name

The **name** of somebody or something is what they are called. *My name is Thomas.*

narrow

Something that is **narrow** does not measure very much from one side to the other. *The road was too narrow for two cars to pass.*

nasty *(nastier nastiest)*

If somebody or something is **nasty**, they are not kind or nice. *What nasty weather!*

natural

Something that is **natural** is made by nature and not by people. Wool is a **natural** material but plastic is not.

nature

1 **Nature** is everything in the world that has not been made by people or machines. Animals, plants and the sea are all part of **nature**, but buildings and cars are not.
2 A person's or an animal's **nature** is what they are like. *Ella has a kind nature.*

naughty *(naughtier naughtiest)*

A child who is **naughty** behaves badly and makes people cross.

near

Something that is **near** is not very far away. *Do you know where the nearest garage is?*

nearly

Nearly means not quite. *Ned can swim nearly as well as his brother.*

neat

Something that is **neat** is tidy and in the right place. *We put the books in neat piles.*

neck

Your **neck** is the part of your body between your head and your shoulders. *Swans and giraffes have long necks.*

necklace

A **necklace** is something pretty, such as a silver chain or beads, that you wear around your neck.

need *(needs needing needed)*

If you **need** something, you must have it. Everybody **needs** sleep to stay healthy.

needle

1 A **needle** is a long pointed piece of metal that you use for sewing. It has a hole at one end for thread to go through.
2 A **needle** is also a long plastic or metal stick that you use for knitting.
3 A **needle** is also one of the thin sharp leaves of trees such as pines.

neighbour

A **neighbour** is somebody who lives near you. *We are good friends with our next-door neighbours.*

nephew

Somebody's **nephew** is the son of their brother or sister.

nervous

If you are **nervous**, you are worried about something that might happen. *My brother was really nervous before his piano exam.*

nest

A **nest** is a home that birds and some other animals build so that their babies can be born there.

net

A **net** is made from string that has been tied together so that there are big holes in between. You can catch fish with one kind of **net**. Games like football, tennis and netball use **nets**.

never

Never means not at any time. *Peter never stops talking.*

new

Something that is **new** has just been made or bought or it has never been used before. *Mum took me shopping to buy a new coat and some new shoes.*

news

News tells you all about what is happening in the world. *We listened to the news on the car radio this morning.*

newspaper

A **newspaper** is sheets of paper folded together with stories and photographs of things that have happened in the world. *Joe is reading today's newspaper.*

next

1 Next means the one that comes after this one. *Next week we go back to school.*
2 Next to means by the side of. *Harry sat next to his uncle.*

nibble *(nibbles nibbling nibbled)*

If you **nibble** something, you eat it by taking tiny bites of it. *The rabbit nibbled the carrot.*

nice

If somebody or something is **nice**, you like them.

niece

Somebody's **niece** is the daughter of their brother or sister.

night

Night is the time when it is dark outside.

nightmare

A **nightmare** is a frightening dream. *I had a nightmare that I was being chased by a hairy monster.*

nod *(nods nodding nodded)*

If you **nod**, you move your head up and down quickly as a way of saying "yes".

noise

A **noise** is a sound that somebody or something makes.

noisy *(noisier noisiest)*

If somebody or something is **noisy**, they make a lot of noise.

noon

Noon is twelve o'clock in the middle of the day. *We met outside the restaurant at noon.*

normal

Something that is **normal** is usual and ordinary. *Cold weather is normal in winter in this country.*

north

North is a direction. If you face the Sun as it rises in the morning, **north** is on your left.

nose

Your **nose** is the part of your face above your mouth and below your eyes. You use your **nose** for breathing and for smelling things.

note

1 A **note** is a short letter. *Billy left a note to say he was going to Jack's house.*

2 A **note** is also one sound in music.

notice

1 *(notices noticing noticed)* If you **notice** something, you see it, hear it or smell it and think about it. *Lola noticed a smell of burning.*
2 A **notice** is a sign with writing on it that tells you something. *The notice on the fence said "Keep out".*

nuisance

A **nuisance** is a person or a thing that keeps annoying you. *We had a nice picnic in the park, but the wasps were a real nuisance.*

number

We use **numbers** when we count. **Numbers** tell us how many things there are.

nurse

A **nurse** is a person who looks after people who are ill or hurt.

nursery

A **nursery** is a place where young children can go in the day to be looked after when they are too young to go to school.

nut

A **nut** is a hard shell with a seed or fruit inside that you can eat. **Nuts** come from trees or plants.

Oo

oar
An **oar** is a long pole with a flat end. You use **oars** for moving a boat through water.

oasis *(oases)*
An **oasis** is a place in a desert where there is water and where plants can grow.

obey *(obeys obeying obeyed)*
When you **obey** somebody, you do what they tell you to do. *We have trained our dog to obey us when we tell her to sit.*

object
An **object** is anything that you can see or touch that is not living. Books, chairs, cups and desks are all **objects**.

obstacle
An **obstacle** is something that gets in your way and stops you doing what you want to do. *There were fallen trees and other obstacles in the road after the storm.*

ocean
An **ocean** is a very very big sea. The Pacific and the Atlantic are both **oceans**.

o'clock
We use **o'clock** to say what time it is. *We go to bed at nine o'clock and get up at half-past seven.*

octopus
(octopuses)
An **octopus** is a sea animal with a soft round body and eight long arms called tentacles. **Octopuses** live at the bottom of the sea. They hide in caves and eat crabs and shellfish.

odd
1 An **odd** number is a number that cannot be divided by 2 without leaving something over. *1, 3, 5, 7 and 9 are odd numbers.*
2 Something that is **odd** is strange. *The computer is making an odd noise.*
3 Odd things do not belong in a pair or a group. *Which thing is the odd one out?*

offer *(offers offering offered)*
If you **offer** to do something or give something, you are ready to do it or give it without being asked. *I offered to take the old lady's dog for a walk.*

office
An **office** is a place where people work. **Offices** have desks, telephones and computers.

officer
An **officer** is an important person in the army or the police who tells people what to do. *Dan's mother is a police officer.*

often
If something happens **often**, it happens many times. *We often go to the park after school if the weather is warm.*

oil
1 Oil is a thick liquid that people burn to make heat and to make engines work. **Oil** comes from the ground or from under the sea.
2 Another kind of **oil** comes from animals and the seeds of plants. We use it for cooking.

old
1 A person who is **old** has lived for many years. *My grandparents are quite old.*
2 Something that is **old** was made a long time ago.
3 Old can also mean the one that you had before. *I like my new coat better than my old one.*

onion
An **onion** is a round vegetable that grows in the ground. **Onions** have a strong taste and smell.

only

Only means no more than. *We only have ten minutes to get ready for the party.*

open

If something is **open**, people or things can go into it or through it. *The gate was open so the sheep got out of the field.*

operation

If somebody has an **operation**, a doctor mends a part of that person's body to make it well.

opinion

Your **opinion** is what you think about somebody or something.

opposite

1 Opposite means different in every way. Young is the **opposite** of old, and good is the **opposite** of bad.

2 Opposite also means on the other side, looking straight at somebody or something. *I sat opposite Sam.*

orange

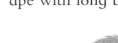

1 An **orange** is a round sweet fruit with a thick skin.

2 Orange is also a colour. You can make it by mixing red and yellow paint.

orchestra

An **orchestra** is a large group of people who play different musical instruments together.

order

1 Order is the way that things are put, one after the other. *The letters of the alphabet are always in the same order.*

2 *(orders ordering ordered)* If somebody **orders** you to do something, they say you must do it. *She ordered us to clear up the mess we had made.*

3 *(orders ordering ordered)* If you **order** something in a restaurant, you say what you want to eat. *My sister and I both ordered cheese and tomato pizzas.*

orang-utan

An **orang-utan** is a large kind of ape with long brown fur.

ordinary

Something that is **ordinary** is not special, different or unusual. *He wore his ordinary clothes to his brother's party.*

organ

1 An **organ** is a large musical instrument like a piano. It has long metal pipes which make different sounds when air passes through them.

2 An **organ** is a part of your body that does a special job. Your heart, your liver and your stomach are **organs**.

ostrich *(ostriches)*

An **ostrich** is a very large bird that lives in Africa. **Ostriches** cannot fly but they run very fast.

otter

An **otter** is an animal with brown fur and a long tail. **Otters** live near water and catch fish to eat.

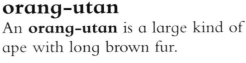

oval

Something that is **oval** is shaped like an egg.

oven

An **oven** is the part like a box inside a cooker, where you bake food. *Bake the cake in a hot oven.*

owe *(owes owing owed)*

If you **owe** money to somebody, you have not yet paid them but you must. *I owe you the £5 that you lent me last week.*

owl

An **owl** is a bird with large eyes that help it to see in the dark. **Owls** hunt small animals, such as mice, at night.

own *(owns owning owned)*

If you **own** something, it is yours. *Do you know who owns that bike?*

P p

pack (packs packing packed)
When you **pack** a bag or box, you put a lot of things inside it. *Jenni packed her bag the night before she went on a school trip.*

package
A **package** is something that you wrap in paper or put in a box or envelope and send.

paddle (paddles paddling paddled)
When you **paddle**, you walk in water at the edge of the sea or in a shallow stream or river. *We took off our shoes and went paddling.*

page
A **page** is one side of a piece of paper. Books and newspapers have **pages**.

pain
Pain is what you feel when a part of your body hurts. *I've got a pain in my leg.*

paint
1 Paint is a coloured liquid that we use to put colour on things such as walls or to make pictures.
2 *(paints painting painted)* When you **paint** something, you use **paint** to put colour on it or to make a picture. *Jane painted her bedroom green and yellow. Connor has painted a picture of his dog.*

painting
A **painting** is a picture that somebody has painted.

pair
1 A **pair** is two things, people or animals that go together. *a pair of shoes.*
2 You can also talk about a **pair** of something, like scissors or trousers, where two parts that are the same have been joined together.

palace
A **palace** is a very big important house. People such as kings, queens and presidents live in palaces. The British Queen lives in Buckingham **Palace**.

pale
Something, such as skin, that is **pale** is almost white. *Her face is very pale - is she feeling all right?*

palm
1 Your **palm** is the inside part of your hand between your wrist and your fingers.
2 A **palm** is also a tree with no branches and big leaves that grow from the top of the trunk. **Palm** trees grow in hot countries.

pan
A **pan** is a metal dish with a long handle. You use **pans** for cooking. *Put some oil in the pan and fry the onion until it is brown.*

pancake
A **pancake** is a kind of very flat round cake. **Pancakes** are made from flour, eggs and milk and cooked in a pan in hot oil.

panda
Pandas are large furry black and white animals that look a bit like bears. **Pandas** live in China but they are now very rare animals.

panic
Panic is sudden fear that you cannot control. *There was panic when the fire alarm went off.*

pant (pants panting panted)
When you **pant**, you breathe quickly with your mouth open. *Penny was panting because she had been running.*

pantomime
A **pantomime** is a kind of play that tells a fairy tale. The actors wear colourful costumes and **pantomimes** have a lot of singing, dancing and jokes.

paper

Paper is a material that we use for writing on and wrapping things in. Books and envelopes are made of **paper**.

parcel

A **parcel** is something wrapped in paper that you can send through the post.

parent

A **parent** is a mother or father.

park

1 A **park** is a place with trees and grass where people can go to enjoy themselves.
2 *(parks parking parked)* When somebody **parks** a car, they leave it somewhere for a time. *Mum parked her car outside the house.*

parrot

A **parrot** is a bird with a curved beak and brightly coloured feathers. Some **parrots** can learn to say a few words.

part

A **part** is one piece of something bigger. *Your fingers are parts of your hand.*

party *(parties)*

A **party** is a time when a group of people meet to have fun together. *Claire is having a party for her birthday.*

pass *(passes passing passed)*

1 If you **pass** somebody or something, you go by them. *Mum usually passes our school on her way to work so she gives us a lift.*
2 If you **pass** something to somebody, you give it to them. *Please pass me the milk.*
3 If you **pass** a test, you do well. *Becky passed all her exams.*

passenger

A **passenger** is a person who is travelling in a car, bus, train, boat or an aeroplane.

past

1 The **past** is time that has already happened. *In the past people did not have computers.*
2 **Past** means after. *Come on - it's past your bedtime.*

paste

Paste is thick wet stuff that you use for sticking things together.

pastry

Pastry is made from flour, fat and water mixed together and rolled flat. You use it to make things such as pies which are baked in the oven.

path

A **path** is a narrow piece of land that you can walk along. *If you follow the path through the woods you won't get lost.*

patient

1 A **patient** is a person who is ill and who is being looked after by a doctor or nurse.
2 A person who is **patient** does not mind waiting a long time for something to happen.

pattern

A **pattern** is the way the shapes and colours are on something. *Harriet's scarf has a pattern of red and yellow spots.*

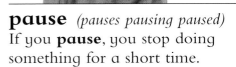

pause *(pauses pausing paused)*

If you **pause**, you stop doing something for a short time.

pavement

A **pavement** is a path at the side of a road where people can walk.

paw

A **paw** is an animal's foot. Cats, dogs and rabbits have **paws**.

pay *(pays paying paid)*

When you **pay** for something, you give money to somebody so that you can have it. *How much did you pay for your lunch?*

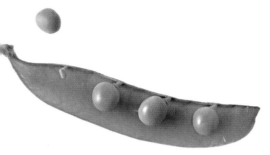

pea
A **pea** is a small round green vegetable that grows in a long covering called a pod.

peace
Peace is a time when everything is quiet and people are not fighting or arguing.

peach *(peaches)*
A **peach** is a soft round fruit. **Peaches** have a yellow and red skin, juicy yellow flesh and a big stone in the middle.

peanut
A **peanut** is a nut that grows under the ground in a thin shell.

pear
A **pear** is a green or yellow fruit that is narrow at the top and big and round at the bottom.

pebble
A **pebble** is a small smooth stone.
The beach was covered with pebbles.

pedal
A **pedal** is a part of a machine that you push with your foot to make the machine work. You press the **pedals** of a bike to make the wheels go round.

peel
1 **Peel** is the skin of some fruit and vegetables. *My little sister will only eat apples if we take off the peel.*
2 *(peels peeling peeled)* If you **peel** a piece of fruit or a vegetable, you take the skin off it. *Ross peeled an orange for me.*

pen
A **pen** is a tool that you use for writing. **Pens** are filled with ink.

pencil
A **pencil** is a thin wooden stick that you use for writing or for drawing pictures.

penguin
A **penguin** is a large black and white bird that can swim but cannot fly. **Penguins** live near oceans in parts of the world where it is very cold.

people
Men, women and children are called **people**.

pepper
1 **Pepper** is a hot-tasting powder that you can put on food. *Pepper can make you sneeze!*
2 A **pepper** is a red, green, yellow or orange vegetable.

person
A **person** is any man, woman or child.

pet
A **pet** is a small animal that you keep in your home. People keep animals such as dogs, cats, rabbits and fish as **pets**. *Do you have any pets? I've got a hamster.*

petal
A **petal** is one of the soft coloured parts of a flower. *Daisies have white petals and a yellow centre.*

petrol
Petrol is a liquid that is made from oil. We use it in cars and lorries to make them go.

phone
Phone is a short word for telephone. *Who's on the phone?*

photograph
A **photograph** is a picture that you take with a camera. We often say photo for short.

piano
A **piano** is a musical instrument with black and white keys that you press with your fingers to make sounds.

pick *(picks picking picked)*
1 When you **pick** something, you choose it because it is the one you want. *Mum helped me pick a nice card for Gran's birthday.*
2 If you **pick** flowers or fruit, you take them with your fingers from where they are growing.
3 If you **pick** something up, you lift it. *Please could you pick up that box for me?*

picnic

A **picnic** is a meal that you take with you to eat outside somewhere nice. *We had a picnic on the beach.*

picture

A **picture** is something that you draw or paint or that you take with a camera.

pie

A **pie** is pastry filled with meat, vegetables or fruit and baked in an oven.

piece

A **piece** is one part of something. *Can I have a small piece of your chocolate cake please?*

pierce *(pierces piercing pierced)*

When a sharp thing **pierces** something, it makes a hole in it. *Sam had her ears pierced.*

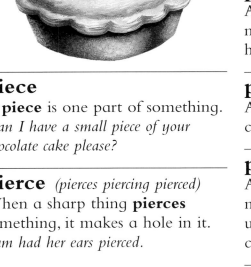

pig

A **pig** is a farm animal that has a fat body, a curly tail and a flat nose called a snout.

pile

A **pile** is a lot of things on top of one another. *Fold your clothes and put them in a neat pile.*

pill

A **pill** is a small round piece of medicine that you swallow.

pillow

A **pillow** is a bag filled with soft material that you put under your head when you are in bed.

pilot

A **pilot** is a person who flies and controls an aeroplane.

pin

A **pin** is a small thin piece of metal with a sharp point. People use **pins** to hold things such as cloth or paper together.

pipe

A **pipe** is a long hollow tube that carries liquids or gas from one place to another.

pirate

A **pirate** is a person who attacks and robs ships at sea. *Jim dressed up as a pirate for the school play.*

pizza

A **pizza** is a flat round kind of bread baked in an oven with things such as tomatoes, cheese, meat and vegetables on top.

place

A **place** is where something is or where something happens.

plain

Something that is **plain** is just one colour with no pattern on it. *a plain blue shirt.*

plan *(plans planning planned)*

If you **plan** something, you think carefully about what you are going to do and how you are going to do it. *We are planning our summer holiday.*

plane

Plane is a short word for aeroplane.

planet

A **planet** is a big round thing in space that moves around a star. Earth is a **planet** that moves around the Sun.

plant

1 A **plant** is a living thing that grows in earth.
2 *(plants planting planted)* When you **plant** flowers, you put them in earth to grow.

plastic

Plastic is a material made in factories. It is used to make a lot of different things such as bottles, bags and toys.

plate

A **plate** is a flat round thing for putting food on.

pocket

A **pocket** is a small bag sewn into your clothes that you can keep things in.
Matt put the ticket in his pocket so that he would not lose it.

pointed

Something that is **pointed** has an end with a sharp point.
She has long pointed fingernails.

poisonous

If you eat something **poisonous**, you become ill or may even die.
Some berries are poisonous and so are some snakes.

pole

A **pole** is a long thin piece of wood or metal. Flags fly on the end of **poles**.

police

The **police** are a group of people who make sure that we obey the law and that everybody is safe.

play

1 *(plays playing played)* When you **play**, you do something for fun. *The children had a good time playing in the snow.*
2 *(plays playing played)* When you **play** a musical instrument, you make music with it. *My brother can play the piano better than I can.*
3 A **play** is a story with people acting in it that you watch in a theatre or on television, or listen to on the radio.

playground

A **playground** is a place where children can play outside.

please

Please is a word that you say when you ask for something. *Please may I have a drink?*

plenty

If there is **plenty** of something, there is more than enough of it. *There is plenty of time before the train goes - let's go and have a cup of coffee.*

plus

We use **plus** to talk about adding one number to another number. We often write **plus** as **+**. *Five plus four is nine (5+4=9).*

poem

A **poem** is a piece of writing that uses words in a special way. The words at the ends of the short lines sometimes rhyme.

poet

A **poet** is a person who writes poems. *William Wordsworth was a famous English poet.*

point

1 A **point** is the sharp end of something. Things such as nails and pins have **points**.
2 A **point** in a game is a score of one.
3 *(points pointing pointed)* When you **point** at something, you lift a finger towards it to show where it is. *Sally pointed out the monkey when she was at the zoo.*

polite

If you are **polite**, you behave well. It is **polite** to say "please" and "thank you".

pond

A **pond** is a small lake. *We fed the ducks on the pond.*

pony *(ponies)*

A **pony** is a kind of small horse.

pool

A **pool** is a place filled with water for swimming in. *Our school has an indoor pool.*

poor

1 A person who is **poor** does not have much money.
2 You sometimes say **poor** when you feel sorry for somebody. *Poor Emily has broken her wrist.*

possible

If something is **possible**, it can be done or it can happen. *It is now possible to travel to the Moon.*

post

1 The **post** is all the letters and parcels that are sent and delivered.
2 A **post** is a strong pole fixed into the ground.
3 *(posts posting posted)* When you **post** a letter or a parcel, you send it to somebody.

pot

A **pot** is a deep round container. Some **pots** are used for cooking, and some for keeping food in. Another kind of **pot** is used for growing plants in.

potato *(potatoes)*

A **potato** is a vegetable that grows under the ground. **Potatatoes** have to be cooked before you can eat them.

pour *(pours pouring poured)*

When you **pour** a liquid, you make it flow from one thing into another. *Sally poured the juice from the jug into a glass.*

powder

Powder is dry stuff that is made up of a lot of very tiny pieces. Flour is a kind of **powder**.

power

Power is the strength to do work or to make something happen. The energy from electricity is one kind of **power**.

practise *(practises practising practised)*

When you **practise** something, you do it again and again until you can do it very well. *We practised throwing the ball very high and catching it.*

prepare *(prepares preparing prepared)*

If you **prepare** something, you get it ready. *We prepared the room for Gran's visit.*

present

1 A **present** is something that you give to somebody. *I got loads of nice presents for my birthday.*
2 The **present** is now. *Mr Smith is not here at present.*

president

A **president** is a person who has been chosen to rule a country that does not have a king or queen.

press *(presses pressing pressed)*

If you **press** something, you push down on it. *You press the keys of a computer to make it work.*

pretend *(pretends pretending pretended)*

When you **pretend**, you try to make people believe something that is not true. *Pretend you're a baby and I'll be your mum.*

pretty *(prettier prettiest)*

A **pretty** person or thing is nice to look at. *What pretty decorations!*

price

The **price** of something is how much money you must pay for it.

prickle

A **prickle** is a sharp point on the skin of some animals and plants. A cactus is covered in **prickles**, and so is a hedgehog.

prime minister

A **prime minister** is a person who has been chosen by the people of a country to lead that country.

prince

A **prince** is the son of a king or queen or of another royal person.

princess *(princesses)*

A **princess** is the daughter of a king, queen or other royal person, or the wife of a prince.

print *(prints printing printed)*

To **print** means to put words and pictures on paper using a machine. *Newspapers, books and magazines are printed.*

prison

A **prison** is a place where some people have to stay when they have done something that is against the law.

prize

A **prize** is something that you win for doing a thing very well. *Jack won first prize for his poem.*

problem

A **problem** is something that is difficult to answer, decide or understand. *My sister has a problem deciding what to wear.*

programme

A **programme** is something that you watch on television or listen to on the radio. *We watched an interesting programme about dinosaurs last night.*

project

If you do a **project** at school, you try to find out all you can about something and then write about it. *Last term we did a project about animals in danger.*

promise *(promises promising promised)*

If you **promise**, you say that you really will or will not do something. *I promise I won't tell anybody your secret.*

protect *(protects protecting protected)*

If you **protect** somebody or something, you keep them safe. *A helmet protects your head when you ride a bike.*

proud

If you are **proud**, you feel really happy about what you or somebody else has done well. *Nancy's mum was very proud of her when she won first prize.*

prove *(proves proving proved)*

When you **prove** something, you show that it is true. *The police cannot prove that he is the thief.*

pudding

Pudding is something sweet that you eat at the end of a meal. *There was apple pie for pudding.*

puddle

A **puddle** is a small pool of water lying on the ground.

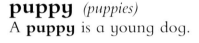

pull *(pulls pulling pulled)*

When you **pull** something, you hold it and move it towards you.

puncture

A **puncture** is a small hole in a tyre that lets the air out. *Our car has got a puncture.*

punish *(punishes punishing punished)*

To **punish** somebody means to do something to them that they do not like because they have done something wrong. *Pete's dad punished him for being naughty by not letting him watch his favourite programme on television.*

pupil

A **pupil** is somebody who is learning at school. *How many pupils are there in your class?*

puppet

A **puppet** is a doll that can be made to move. Some **puppets** have strings that you pull. Others are moved by putting your hand inside and moving your fingers.

puppy *(puppies)*

A **puppy** is a young dog.

pure

Something that is **pure** is not mixed with anything else. *This is pure apple juice.*

push *(pushes pushing pushed)*

When you **push** something, you move it away from you using your hands.

puzzle

A **puzzle** is a game or question that is fun to try to work out. *Clara is doing a jigsaw puzzle.*

pyjamas

Pyjamas are trousers and a shirt that you can wear in bed.

Qq

quack
A **quack** is the loud sound that a duck makes.

quality
Quality is how good or bad something is.

quantity
A **quantity** is how much there is, or how many there are of something. *a huge quantity of food.*

quarrel *(quarrels quarrelling quarrelled)*
When people **quarrel**, they talk in an angry way to one another because they do not agree about something. *Ben and his brother are always quarrelling.*

quarry
A quarry is a place where people dig stone out of the ground to use for building and other things.

quarter
A **quarter** is one of four equal parts of something. *We divided the pizza into quarters because there were four of us.*

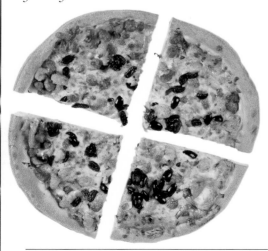

quay
A **quay** is a place in a harbour where boats can be tied up.

queen
A **queen** is a woman who is the ruler of a country or who is the wife of a king. *Some playing cards have pictures of a queen on them.*

question
When you ask a **question**, you want to find out about something.

question mark
A **question mark** is the sign ? that you write at the end of a sentence to show that somebody has asked a question.

queue
A **queue** is a line of people waiting for something. *There are long queues at the post office every Friday morning.*

quiche
A **quiche** is a kind of pie without a pastry top and filled with things made from eggs, cheese, onion, ham and tomatoes.

quick
1 If somebody or something is **quick**, they move fast. *Be quick or you'll be late.*
2 Something that is **quick** is done in a short time. *I just need to make a quick phone call.*

quiet
If somebody or something is **quiet**, they make only a little noise or no noise at all. *Ssh, please be quiet. The baby is asleep.*

quilt
A **quilt** is a thick soft cover on a bed to keep you warm. Some quilts are filled with feathers. *Lucy is hiding under her quilt.*

quit *(quits quitting quit or quitted)*
If you **quit** you leave or stop doing something. *Don't forget to quit the program before you turn off the computer.*

quite
1 **Quite** means more than a little bit. *It's quite a good film but not as good as the book.*
2 **Quite** can also mean really. *I'm not quite sure how to spell the word. I'll look in the dictionary.*

quiz *(quizzes)*
A **quiz** is a test or game in which people show how much they know by trying to answer a lot of questions about something.

quote
If you **quote** something, you say words that were said or written by somebody else before. *David quoted a line from the film he had seen.*

Rr

rabbit
A **rabbit** is a small furry animal with long ears. **Rabbits** live in holes under the ground.

race
A **race** is a way of finding out who or what can go the fastest. *Which horse won the race?*

radio
You can listen to music, the news or other programmes on a **radio**. **Radios** are machines that bring sounds through the air.

raft
A **raft** is a kind of flat boat. Some **rafts** are made from pieces of wood joined together.

rail
1 **Rails** are the long metal bars that trains travel along.
2 A **rail** is also a long metal bar that you can hold on to.

railway
A **railway** is a kind of path made of rails that trains travel along.

rain
1 **Rain** is the drops of water that fall from clouds.
2 (rains raining rained) When it **rains**, drops of water fall from the clouds. *It rained everyday last week.*

rainbow
A **rainbow** is a curved shape of different colours that you sometimes see in the sky after it has rained. It is made by the sun shining through rain.

raise *(raises raising raised)*
If you **raise** something, you lift it up. *Katie raised her hand.*

rake
A **rake** is a tool with a long handle and a row of sharp points at one end. You use a **rake** in the garden for collecting leaves and grass together or for making the earth smooth.

ran
Look at **run**.
Tom ran out into the garden.

rang
Look at **ring**.
Who rang the bell?

rare
Something that is **rare** is not seen or found very often, or it does not happen very often. *Black pandas are rare animals.*

rat
A **rat** is an animal with sharp teeth that looks like a big mouse.

raw
Raw food is not cooked. You eat **raw** lettuce in salads.

reach *(reaches reaching reached)*
1 If you **reach** for something, you stretch out your hand to touch it or hold it.
2 When you **reach** a place, you arrive there. *We reached the island by boat.*

read *(reads reading read)*
When you **read**, you look at words and know what they mean. *You are reading these words.*

ready
If somebody is **ready**, they can do something straight away.

real
Something that is **real** is true or it is not a copy. *Is that a real frog or a toy one?*

realize *(realizes realizing realized)*
If you **realize** something, you suddenly understand or know it. *When I got closer I realized the man was my next-door neighbour.*

really
1 **Really** means that something is true. *Is she really asleep or is she just pretending?*
2 **Really** also means very. *It was a really good party.*

reason

A **reason** for something tells us why it happened. *She had a good reason for being late - she had to go to the doctor's.*

record

1 A **record** is the fastest or the best that has ever been done. *He broke the world record for the high jump in the Olympic Games.*

2 A **record** is also a flat round piece of plastic with music or other sounds on it. You put **records** on a record-player to listen to them. *Put on another record.*

reflection

A **reflection** is what you see when you look into shiny things such as mirrors.

refrigerator

A **refrigerator** is a metal box with a machine inside it that keeps food and drink cold and fresh. It is often called a fridge for short. *Put the milk in the refrigerator.*

refuse *(refuses refusing refused)*

If you **refuse**, you say you will not do something that somebody has asked you to do. *Charlie refused to take the dog for a walk.*

register

A **register** is a book with a list of the names of all the pupils in a class. *The teacher opened the register.*

remember *(remembers remembering remembered)*

If you **remember** something, you bring it back into your mind. *Can you remember when Tom's birthday is?*

remind *(reminds reminding reminded)*

If you **remind** somebody of something, you help them to remember it. *Remind me to buy a birthday card tomorrow.*

repair *(repairs repairing repaired)*

If you **repair** something that is broken, you mend it.

repeat *(repeats repeating repeated)*

If you **repeat** something, you say it or do it again. *Could you please repeat what you just said?*

reply *(replies replying replied)*

When you **reply**, you give an answer. *He replied to my letter.*

reptile

A **reptile** is an animal with cold blood. Most **reptiles** have skin covered in scales. **Reptiles** lay eggs. Crocodiles, lizards, snakes and tortoises are all **reptiles**.

rescue *(rescues rescuing rescued)*

If you **rescue** somebody, you help them escape from danger. *We helped to rescue a cat which was stuck up a tree.*

rest

1 *(rests resting rested)* When you **rest**, you stop what you are doing and sit or lie down quietly for a time. *She's resting because she's tired.*

2 The **rest** is what is left after everything or everybody else has gone. *She ate some of her dinner and gave the rest to the dog!*

restaurant

A **restaurant** is a place where you can go to buy and eat meals.

result

1 A **result** is something that happens because of something else. *The road was flooded as a result of all the rain.*

2 A **result** is also the goals or points at the end of a game. *We listen to the football results on the radio on Saturday evenings.*

return *(returns returning returned)*

1 When you **return**, you go back. *We had a new teacher when we returned to school after the holidays.*

2 If you **return** something that you have borrowed, you give it back. *I have to return these books to the library tomorrow.*

reward

A **reward** is something nice that somebody gives you because of something good you have done. *We were taken to see a film as a reward for helping Mum tidy the cupboards.*

rhinoceros *(rhinoceroses)*

A **rhinoceros** is a very big wild animal with thick skin. It has one or two horns on its nose. **Rhinoceroses** live in Africa and Asia. They are often called rhinos for short.

rhyme (rhymes rhyming rhymed)
Words that **rhyme** have the same sound at the end. *The word "rice" rhymes with "mice", and "cat" rhymes with "hat".*

ribbon
A **ribbon** is a long thin piece of coloured cloth. *Jessie wore pink ribbons in her hair.*

rice
Rice is a food that comes from the small white seeds of a plant.

rich
People who are **rich** have a lot of money and expensive things.

riddle
A **riddle** is a question or puzzle that is hard to work out and that has a clever answer, such as: *"What has hands but no arms?" Answer: "A clock".*

ride
1 (rides riding rode ridden) When you **ride** a bike or horse, you sit on it as it goes along.

2 A **ride** is a journey in something like a car or bus.

right
1 If something is **right**, there are no mistakes. *That was the right answer.*
2 **Right** is the opposite of left. *When you read a line of writing, you start on the left-hand side and finish on the right.*

ring
1 A **ring** is a circle of metal that you wear on your finger.
2 A **ring** is also a circle. *She drew a ring in chalk on the ground and jumped into it.*
3 (rings ringing rang rung) If something **rings**, it makes a sound like a bell. *Did somebody ring the doorbell?*

ripe
When fruit is **ripe**, it is ready to eat. *Let's go and pick the strawberries now they are ripe.*

rise (rises rising rose risen)
When something **rises**, it goes up. *The Sun rises in the sky in the East every morning.*

river
A **river** is a lot of moving water that flows through a country. **Rivers** flow into the sea or into a lake. *The River Ganges is in India.*

road
A **road** is a wide path that cars, bicycles, buses and lorries travel along between one town, city or village and another.

roar (roars roaring roared)
To **roar** is to make a loud noise like the sound that wild animals such as lions and tigers make. *A motorbike roared past.*

rob (robs robbing robbed)
To **rob** means to take things that do not belong to you. *The two men who robbed the supermarket have been caught by the police and have been sent to prison.*

robin
A **robin** is a small bird with red feathers on its chest.

robot
A **robot** is a machine that can do some of the jobs that people do. Some factories use **robots** to make things such as cars.

rock
1 **Rock** is the hard stuff that mountains are made of.
2 (rocks rocking rocked) If something **rocks**, it moves from side to side very gently.

rocket
A **rocket** is a big machine like a metal tube that is used to send spacecraft into space. *The film began with a big rocket lifting-off into space.*

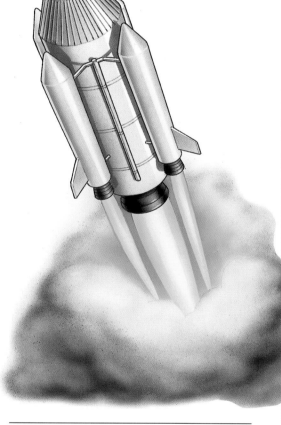

rode Look at **ride**.
I rode on Sam's new bike.

roll
1 (rolls rolling rolled) When something **rolls**, it moves by turning over and over. *The ball rolled under the table.*
2 A **roll** is a long piece of something that has been wrapped around itself many times. *a roll of tape.*
3 A **roll** is also a small round piece of bread made for one person.

roller skate

Roller skates are boots with wheels on the bottom for skating over smooth hard ground.

roof

A **roof** is the part that covers the top of a building or a vehicle such as a car.

room

A **room** is one of the spaces inside a building. **Rooms** have walls, a ceiling and a door. *The room you sleep in is called a bedroom and the room where you prepare food is called a kitchen.*

root

A **root** is the part of a plant that grows under the ground. Plants and trees get food and water through their **roots**.

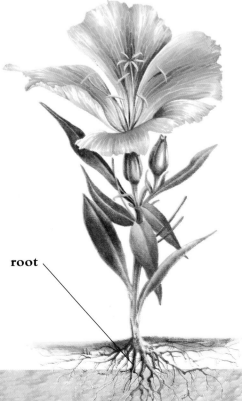

root

rope

Rope is strong thick string for lifting and pulling things. *We tied a rope to the boat and pulled it up onto the river bank.*

rose

1 A **rose** is a flower with a nice smell. Some **roses** have sharp pointed parts called thorns on their stems.
2 Look at **rise**. *The Sun rose above the mountains.*

rotten

Something that is **rotten** has gone bad or is spoilt. *You cannot eat that apple because it is rotten.*

rough

1 Something that feels **rough** is not smooth. The bark of a tree feels **rough**.

2 If somebody is **rough**, they are not gentle. *Don't be too rough when you play in the park with the puppy.*

round

Something that is **round** has no corners and has the same shape as a circle or a ball.

roundabout

1 A **roundabout** is a kind of island where different roads meet. Traffic has to go around a **roundabout** in a circle.

2 A **roundabout** is also a large machine at a fair that children can have a ride on as it goes round and round.

rounders

Rounders is a game for two teams that is played outdoors with a bat and ball. *We played rounders in the park.*

row

1 A **row** is a line of people or things. *Jennifer planted a row of flowers in the front garden.*
2 *(rows rowing rowed)* When you **row** a boat, you move it along by using oars. *Dad said he will take us rowing on Sunday.*

royal

Royal means belonging to a king and queen or their family. *a royal palace.*

rub *(rubs rubbing rubbed)*
If you **rub** things together, you move them against each other. *Megan rubbed her hands together to warm them up.*

rubber

1 Rubber is a strong material that stretches and bends easily and bounces. Tyres, balls and gloves can all be made from **rubber**. *Mum wears yellow rubber gloves for washing-up.*

2 A **rubber** is something made from a small piece of **rubber** that can make pencil marks disappear.

rubbish

Rubbish is anything that you do not want and that you throw away, such as old paper and empty cans. *Our rubbish gets collected every Wednesday.*

ruby *(rubies)*

A **ruby** is a red jewel. **Rubies** cost a lot of money. *My aunt has a very expensive ruby ring.*

rudder

A **rudder** is a flat piece of wood or metal at the back of a ship or aircraft that makes the ship or aircraft move to the left or right.

rude

A person who is **rude** behaves in a bad way and does not think about other people's feelings.

rug

A **rug** is a thick piece of cloth that you put on the floor. It is like a small carpet.

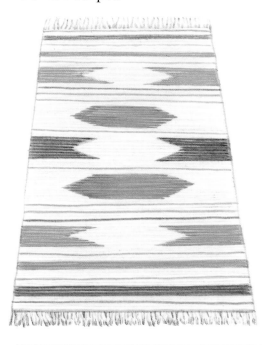

rugby

Rugby is a game played by two teams using an oval-shaped ball.

ruin

A **ruin** is what is left of a building when most of it has fallen down and been destroyed.

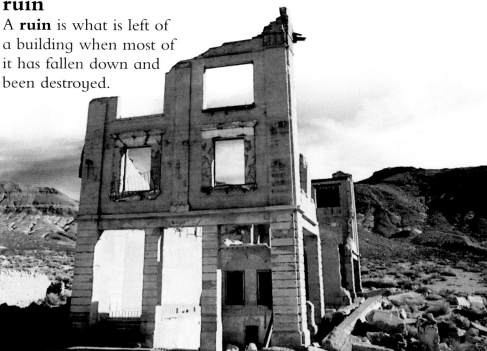

rule

1 **Rules** tell you what you must do and what you must not do. Games have **rules**.
2 *(rules ruling ruled)* To **rule** means to lead and control a country and all the people who live there. *Queen Victoria ruled for many years.*

ruler

1 A **ruler** is a long piece of wood, plastic or metal that you use to help you draw straight lines or for measuring how long something is.
2 A **ruler** is also a person who rules a country.

rumble *(rumbles rumbling rumbled)*

To **rumble** is to make a long low sound like thunder. *The traffic rumbled past all night.*

run *(runs running ran run)*

When you **run**, you move your legs very quickly to get somewhere. *Nick ran in the race but he came last!*

runny

If something is **runny**, it flows like a liquid. *The honey you gave me is very runny.*

rung Look at ring.

I've rung the bell twice but there's nobody at home.

runway

A **runway** is a long piece of flat ground where aircraft can take off and land.

rush *(rushes rushing rushed)*

If you **rush**, you go somewhere or do something very quickly. *Tyrone rushed home to tell his dad the good news.*

rustle *(rustles rustling rustled)*

When something **rustles**, it makes the soft sound of dry leaves moving about in the wind.

rusty

If something is **rusty**, it is covered in brown stuff that spreads on some metals when they get wet.

rye

Rye is a plant that grows on farms. It can be used to make flour.

Ss

sad (sadder saddest)
When you are **sad**, you feel unhappy. *Harry felt sad when his hamster died.*

safe
If you are **safe**, you are not in any danger.

sail
A **sail** is a large piece of cloth on a boat. When the wind blows against the **sail**, the boat moves along. *The boat has a red-striped sail.*

sailor
A **sailor** is a person who works on a boat.

salad
A **salad** is a mixture of cold vegetables and other things.

salt
Salt is a white powder that people put on their food to give it more taste. **Salt** is found in the earth and in sea water.

same
If two things are the **same**, they are like each other in every way. *Lauren and her sister sound the same on the phone.*

sand
Sand is a kind of powder made of tiny pieces of rock. **Sand** covers deserts and some beaches. *I love playing in the sand.*

sandwich
A **sandwich** is two pieces of bread with cheese, meat or some other food in between.

sang Look at **sing**.
He sang on his own in front of the whole school.

sank Look at **sink**.
The ship sank all the way to the bottom of the ocean.

sat Look at **sit**.
We sat down to eat our dinner at eight o' clock last night.

satellite
1 A **satellite** is an object that moves around a planet in space.
2 A **satellite** is also a machine that moves around in space and sends information back to earth about things like the weather.

saucepan
A **saucepan** is a metal pot with a long handle and a lid. You use a **saucepan** for cooking.

saucer
A **saucer** is a small plate that you put a cup on.

save (saves saving saved)
1 If you **save** somebody, you take them away from danger. *She saved the boy from falling into the river.*
2 If you **save** money, you do not spend it but keep it somewhere for another time. *Millie is saving all her money to buy a new pair of roller-skates.*

saw
1 A **saw** is a tool for cutting hard materials such as wood. It has a metal blade with sharp points called teeth on one edge.
2 Look at **see**.
I saw that film before my friend did.

say (says saying said)
When you **say** something, you make words with your mouth. *I can't hear what you're saying because it's too noisy in here.*

scale
A **scale** is one of the small thin shiny pieces that cover the skin of fish and reptiles. *The fishes' scales were shining in the sunlight.*

scales
Scales are a machine that we use to find out how heavy somebody or something is. *Step on the scales and I'll weigh you.*

scare *(scares scaring scared)*
If something **scares** you, it makes you feel frightened.

scarf *(scarves)*
A **scarf** is a long piece of cloth that you wear around your neck.

school
A **school** is a place where children go to learn all sorts of different things from teachers.

science
Science is something that we learn about at school. **Science** teaches us about things like plants and animals, the Earth and the planets, and how things work.

scissors
A pair of **scissors** is a tool for cutting. It has two blades joined together in the middle.

score
1 The **score** is the number of points each side has in a game. *The score at half time was 3-2.*
2 *(scores scoring scored)* To **score** is to get a point or goal in a game. *Our team scored just before the end of the match.*

scratch *(scratches scratching scratched)*
1 When you **scratch** something, you rub something sharp against it. *Jamie scratched his head.*
2 To **scratch** also means to damage a thing with something sharp. *Our cat is always scratching the furniture with his claws.*

scream *(screams screaming screamed)*
If you **scream**, you shout in a very loud high voice. People **scream** when they are afraid, angry or hurt.

screen
A **screen** is a flat surface on which you see films and television programmes. Computers also have **screens**.

sea
A **sea** is a large area of salt water. **Seas** cover large parts of the Earth.

seal
A **seal** is a furry animal that lives in the sea and on land. Many **seals** live in icy waters.

search *(searches searching searched)*
When you **search** for something, you try to find it by looking very carefully. *We've searched everywhere for your keys.*

seaside
The **seaside** is the land next to the sea. *We went to the seaside for our holidays.*

season
A **season** is one of the four parts of a year. The **seasons** are spring, summer, autumn and winter.

seat
A **seat** is anything that you can sit on. *There are plenty of seats on the train.*

second
1 A **second** is a very short amount of time. There are sixty **seconds** in a minute.
2 **Second** also means next after the first. *I was the second person to arrive at the party.*

secret
A **secret** is something that you do not want anybody to know about. *I can't tell you where they have gone - it's a secret.*

see *(sees seeing saw seen)*
When you **see** something, you find out about it with your eyes.

seed
A **seed** is a tiny part of a plant. You put **seeds** into the ground, and new plants grow from them.

seem *(seems seeming seemed)*
To **seem** means to look or feel like something. *The puppies seem to be happy in their new homes.*

seen Look at **see**.
Have you ever seen a ghost?

shape

The **shape** of something is the way that its outside edges make a pattern. A circle is a round **shape**.

seesaw

A **seesaw** is a kind of toy for two people to play on. It has a long flat part that they sit on, one at each end, to go up and down.

selfish

Selfish people only think about themselves and do not care about other people.

sell *(sells selling sold)*

If somebody **sells** you something, they give it to you and you give them money for it. *My dad sold his car to a friend.*

send *(sends sending sent)*

When you **send** something somewhere, you make it go there. *I sent a birthday card and present in the post to my aunt.*

sensible

If you are **sensible**, you think carefully about what you are going to do and you do not do anything silly. *We can go to the fair as long as we are sensible, Mum said.*

sentence

A **sentence** is a group of words. A **sentence** starts with a capital letter (such as A, F or T) and ends with a full stop.

set

A **set** is a group of things that belong together. *We gave granddad a set of gardening tools as a present.*

settee

A **settee** is a long soft chair for two or more people to sit on. *Our settee at home is dark blue.*

sew *(sews sewing sewed sewn)*

When you **sew**, you use a needle and thread to join pieces of cloth together, or to fix things to cloth. *Zoe is sewing a button on her shirt.*

shadow

A **shadow** is a dark shape that a person or thing makes when they are blocking out the light. *It was too hot for us to sit in the sun so we sat in the shadow of the big oak tree.*

shake *(shakes shaking shook shaken)*

When you **shake** something, you move it quickly up and down or from side to side. *Shake the medicine before you open the bottle.*

shallow

Water that is **shallow** is not very deep. *We can paddle here - the river is quite shallow.*

share *(shares sharing shared)*

When you **share** something, you give a part of it to another person. *She shared her sandwiches with her friend.*

shark

A **shark** is large sea fish with sharp teeth. Some **sharks** are very fierce.

sharp

Something that is **sharp** has a point or thin edge that can cut things easily. *Be careful with that knife - it's really sharp.*

shave *(shaves shaving shaved)*

When a man **shaves**, he cuts the hair that grows on his face with a sharp tool called a razor.

shed

A **shed** is a small wooden building. *Ben keeps his bike in the shed at the end of the garden.*

sheep *(sheep)*

A **sheep** is a farm animal. We get wool and meat from **sheep**. *There are a lot of sheep in that field.*

sheet

1 A **sheet** is a large piece of thin cloth that you put on a bed.
2 A **sheet** is also a thin flat piece of something such as plastic, paper or glass.

shelf *(shelves)*

A **shelf** is a long flat piece of wood or metal fixed to a wall. You put things on **shelves** to keep them tidy or so that people can see them.

shell

A **shell** is the hard outside covering of things such as eggs, nuts and some animals. Snails and tortoises have **shells**. You can sometimes find the **shells** of some sea animals on the beach.

shine *(shines shining shone)*

Something that **shines** gives out light, or it is smooth and bright like gold or silver. *We polished the silver cup until it shone.*

shiny *(shinier shiniest)*

If something is **shiny**, it shines. *She had a shiny new car.*

ship

A **ship** is a big boat that goes on the sea.

shirt

A **shirt** is something that you wear on the top part of your body. **Shirts** have sleeves, buttons, and usually a collar.

shiver *(shivers shivering shivered)*

If you **shiver**, you shake because you are cold or afraid. *Jake was shivering when he got out of the pool.*

shoe

Shoes are what you wear on your feet to keep them warm and dry.

shone Look at **shine**. *The sun shone brightly all day.*

shook Look at **shake**. *He shook his head.*

shoot *(shoots shooting shot)*

To **shoot** means to send something out very fast from a gun or a bow. You **shoot** arrows from a bow, and you **shoot** bullets from a gun. *I was upset at the end of the film when he got shot.*

shop

A **shop** is a place where you can buy things. *A really good shop has just opened in town.*

shore

The **shore** is the land along the edge of the sea or a very large lake. *We collected shells at the seashore.*

short

1 A **short** time or distance is not very long. *It's only a short journey from my house to Bob's.*
2 Somebody or something that is **short** is not tall or long. *My little sister is much too short to reach the top drawer of the chest of drawers.*

shot Look at **shoot**. *He shot the arrow at the tree.*

shoulder

Your **shoulder** is the top part of your body between your neck and the top part of your arm. *The little boy sat on his dad's shoulders.*

shout *(shouts shouting shouted)*

If you **shout**, you speak in a very loud voice. *She shouted to me across the room.*

show

1 *(shows showing showed)* When you **show** something, you let people see it. *Alice showed me the painting that she did at school today.*
2 *(shows showing showed)* If you **show** somebody how to do something, you teach them how to do it. *Jane showed me what to do.*
3 A **show** is something with singing or dancing that you can watch in the theatre or on the television. *Did you enjoy the show?*

shower

1 A **shower** is something that you stand under to wash yourself with a spray of water.

2 A **shower** is also rain or snow that falls for a short time. *The rain has stopped now - it was only a quick shower.*

shrink *(shrinks shrinking shrank shrunk)*

If something **shrinks**, it gets smaller. *The shirt shrank when I washed it.*

shut *(shuts shutting shut)*

When you **shut** something such as a box or a door, you move it so that it is not open. *Please shut all the doors and windows before you go out. You shut your eyes before you go to sleep.*

shy

If you are **shy**, you do not like meeting and talking to people that you do not know.

side

1 The **side** of something is the left or the right of it.

2 The **sides** of something such as a box are its flat surfaces. *Dice have six sides.*

3 The **sides** of something are also its edges. *A triangle has three sides.*

4 The **sides** in a game are the groups or teams that are playing against each other.

sight

Sight is being able to see. *My granddad wears glasses because his sight is not very good.*

sign

1 A **sign** is a notice with words or drawings that tells people something. *The arrow on the sign says: Turn right.*

2 *(signs signing signed)* When you **sign** something, you write your name on it.

silence

Silence is when there is no sound at all.

silk

Silk is a smooth shiny material. It is made from threads that are spun by insects called silkworms.

silly *(sillier silliest)*

1 If somebody or something is **silly**, they are funny and make us laugh. *He wore a silly hat.*

2 **Silly** can also mean not sensible. *It was a bit silly of you to go out in the rain with no shoes on.*

silver

Silver is a shiny grey metal that is used for making things such as rings and necklaces.

sing *(sings singing sang sung)*

When you **sing**, you use your voice to make music.

sink

1 A **sink** is the place in a kitchen where you wash dishes.

2 *(sinks sinking sank sunk)* When something **sinks**, it goes down under water. *The pebble sank to the bottom of the pond.*

sip *(sips sipping sipped)*

If you **sip** something, you drink a tiny amount at a time.

sister

Your **sister** is a girl or woman who has the same mother and father as you.

sit *(sits sitting sat)*

When you **sit**, you put your bottom on something. *We sat on the bench in the park.*

size

The **size** of something is how big it is. *What size shoes do you take?*

skate

1 Ice **skates** are special boots with blades underneath that you wear for sliding on ice.

2 Roller **skates** are special boots with little wheels underneath for moving on flat ground.

skateboard

A **skateboard** is a board with wheels on the bottom. You ride it by standing on it with one foot and pushing the ground with the other foot.

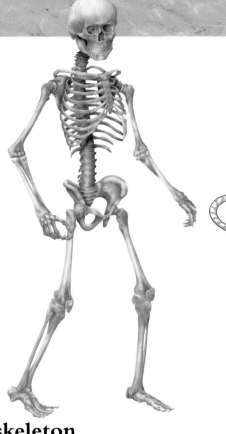

skeleton
A **skeleton** is all the bones that are inside the body of a person or an animal.

ski
Skis are long pieces of metal, plastic or wood that you wear on your feet with special boots to move quickly on snow.

skin
Skin is what covers the bodies of people and animals. Fruit and vegetables also have **skin**.

skip *(skips skipping skipped)*
When you **skip**, you move along by jumping from one foot to the other. You can also **skip** with a skipping rope.

skirt
A **skirt** is something that girls and women wear. It hangs down from the waist and covers the bottom part of the body.

sky *(skies)*
The **sky** is all the space above the Earth. You can see the Moon and stars in the **sky**.

skyscraper
A **skyscraper** is a building that is so tall that it looks as if it is touching the sky.

sledge
A **sledge** is something that you sit on to ride over snow. It has two long pieces of wood on the bottom to help it slide along.

sleep *(sleeps sleeping slept)*
When you **sleep**, you close your eyes and your body rests. *John slept well because he was very tired after his long journey.*

sleeve
A **sleeve** is the part of something such as a shirt or jacket that covers your arm.

slice
A **slice** is a thin piece that has been cut from something. *Can I have a slice of cake, please?*

slide
1 *(slides sliding slid)* When something **slides**, it moves smoothly over a surface. *Ella fell and slid on her bottom across the floor.*
2 A **slide** is something that you play on. It has steps on one side that you climb up and a long piece of slippery metal on the other side that you **slide** down.

slip *(slips slipping slipped)*
When you **slip**, you slide and fall down. *Thomas nearly slipped on the wet floor.*

slipper
Slippers are soft shoes that you wear indoors.

slippery
When something is **slippery**, it is so smooth or wet that you cannot hold it or walk on it easily. *Be careful - the step is a bit slippery after the rain.*

slow
Something that is **slow** does not move very quickly.

small
Something that is **small** is not large. *Mice are small creatures.*

smash *(smashes smashing smashed)*
If you **smash** something by hitting or dropping it, it breaks into lots of small pieces. *He threw the ball too hard and it smashed a window.*

smell *(smells smelling smelt or smelled)*
1 When you **smell** something, you notice it with your nose. *Dogs can smell things from a long way away.*
2 When something **smells**, you can find out about it using your nose. *That cake smells lovely.*

smile *(smiles smiling smiled)*
When you **smile**, the corners of your mouth turn up. People **smile** when they are happy.

smoke

Smoke is the grey or black cloud that goes up into the air when something is on fire.

smooth

If something is **smooth**, you cannot feel any rough parts on it when you touch it. *The top of the table is shiny and smooth.*

snail

A **snail** is a small creature with a soft body that lives inside a shell. **Snails** move very slowly.

snake

A **snake** is a reptile with a long thin body and no legs. **Snakes** move along the ground by sliding. Some **snakes** bite and are dangerous.

sneeze *(sneezes sneezing sneezed)*

When you **sneeze**, air suddenly blows out of your nose and mouth making a loud noise. You **sneeze** when you have a cold. *The pepper made me sneeze.*

snow

Snow is soft pieces of white frozen water that falls from the sky when it is very cold.

soap

Soap is something that we use with water for washing.

sock

Socks are soft coverings that you wear on your feet inside your shoes.

soft

If something is **soft**, it is not hard.

soil

Soil is the brown stuff that plants grow in. *I filled the pot with soil and planted some seeds in it.*

sold Look at **sell**.
The shop sold all kinds of toys.

soldier

A **soldier** is a person who is in an army and who is trained to fight in a war.

solid

1 Something that is **solid** is hard and does not change its shape. *Water is liquid and ice is solid.*
2 A **solid** object is not hollow. *That table is made of solid wood.*

son

A **son** is a boy or man who is somebody's child.

song

A **song** is a piece of music with words that you sing.

soon

If something is going to happen **soon**, it will happen in a very short time from now. *We'll soon be home.*

sore

If a part of your body feels **sore**, it hurts a little. *I've got a sore throat.*

sorry

If you are **sorry**, you feel sad because you wish that something had not happened. *I'm really sorry I shouted at you. I didn't mean to upset you.*

sort

1 A **sort** is a kind. *What sort of music do you like?*
2 *(sorts sorting sorted)* When you **sort** things, you put them into groups. *Emily is sorting the bricks into different colours.*

sound

A **sound** is anything that you can hear. *He heard the sound of somebody coming up the stairs.*

soup

Soup is a hot liquid food that you eat with a spoon. **Soup** is made from things like vegetables and meat.

sour

Something that is **sour** has a taste that is not sweet, like the kind of taste that a lemon has.

south

South is a direction. If you face the Sun as it rises in the morning, **south** is on your right.

space

1 Space is a place that is empty. *Can you find a space to park?*
2 Space is also everything far above the Earth where the planets and stars are.

spaceship

A **spaceship** is a vehicle that travels in space.

spade

A **spade** is a tool with a long handle and a wider flat part at the end that you use for digging.

speak *(speaks speaking spoke spoken)*

When you **speak**, you say words.

special

1 Something that is **special** is not ordinary but is important and better than the usual kind. *Birthdays are special days.*

2 Special also means made to do a job. *You need a special tool for cutting glass - you can't use a knife!*

speed

Speed is how fast something moves or happens. *Some aircrafts like Concorde travel faster than the speed of sound.*

spell

1 *(spells spelling spelt or spelled)* When you **spell** a word, you put letters in the right order. *"How do you spell 'rough'?" "R-O-U-G-H."*
2 A **spell** is a magic rhyme or trick in fairy stories that makes something happen. *The wicked witch put a spell on the girl and turned her into a frog.*

spend *(spends spending spent)*

1 When you **spend** money, you use it to pay for something. *How much money have you spent?*
2 When you **spend** time doing something, you use your time to do it. *We spent the whole day playing in the garden.*

spider

A **spider** is a small creature with eight legs and no wings. **Spiders** spin webs in which they catch insects to eat.

spill *(spills spilling spilt or spilled)*

If you **spill** something, you make it flow out by mistake. *Ian spilt his orange juice on the kitchen floor.*

spin *(spins spinning spun)*

1 When something **spins**, it goes round and round. *The Earth spins as it travels around the Sun.*
2 To **spin** also means to pull and twist something such as cotton or wool into long threads.

spine

Your **spine** is the long line of bones down the centre of your back.

splash *(splashes splashing splashed)*

When you **splash** a liquid, you make drops of it fly around to make things wet. *I took a shower and the water splashed on the floor.*

spoil *(spoils spoiling spoilt or spoiled)*

If you **spoil** something, you make it less good than it was before. *The rain spoiled our picnic.*

spoke, spoken Look at **speak**.

He spoke very clearly. I have never spoken to her before.

spooky *(spookier spookiest)*
If something is **spooky**, it is strange and frightening. *The old house felt really spooky.*

spoon
A **spoon** is something that you use for picking up food with. It has a handle at one end and a round part at the other end.

sport
A **sport** is a game or something else that you do to keep your body fit. Many **sports** are played outside. Swimming, tennis and football are all **sports**.

spot
1 A **spot** is a small round mark on something. *The teapot has lots of white spots.*

2 A **spot** is also a small red mark on your skin.

spray
A **spray** is a lot of very small drops of liquid that shoot out of something.

spread *(spreads spreading spread)*
1 When you **spread** something, you make it cover a surface. *She spread jam on the bread.*
2 When a bird **spreads** its wings, it opens them out as far as possible. *The eagle spread its wings and flew away.*

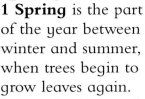

spring
1 **Spring** is the part of the year between winter and summer, when trees begin to grow leaves again.
2 A **spring** is a curly piece of metal that goes back into the same shape after you have pressed or stretched it.
3 *(springs springing sprang sprung)* To **spring** means to jump. *The fox sprang over the fence.*

spun Look at **spin**.
The spider has spun a web.

square
A **square** is a shape with four corners and four sides that are all the same length.

squash *(squashes squashing squashed)*
If you **squash** something you press it hard so that it becomes flat. *She sat down on the cake and squashed it.*

squeak *(squeaks squeaking squeaked)*
If something **squeaks** it makes a short high sound, something like the sound that a mouse makes. *The brakes on my bike squeak.*

squeeze *(squeezes squeezing squeezed)*
If you **squeeze** something, you hold and press it hard on the sides. *She squeezed my hand so hard that it hurt.*

squirrel
A **squirrel** is a small furry animal with a thick tail. **Squirrels** usually live in trees, and they eat nuts.

stable
A **stable** is a building where horses are kept.

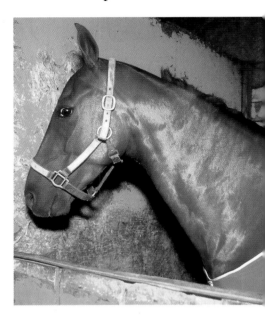

stairs
Stairs are a set of steps inside a building. *We walked up the stairs to the third floor.*

stamp
A **stamp** is a small piece of paper that you stick on a letter to show that you have paid to post it.

stand *(stands standing stood)*
When you **stand** somewhere, you are on your feet without moving.

star
1 A **star** is one of the bright lights that you see at night when the sky is clear. **Stars** are millions and millions of kilometres away from us.
2 A **star** is also a shape with five or six points.

stare *(stares staring stared)*
When you **stare** at somebody or something, you look at them for a long time without moving your eyes. *Tim was staring at the woman because he was trying hard to remember her name.*

start *(starts starting started)*
When you **start** to do something, you do the first part of it. *I started to read you a story but you fell asleep before I had finished.*

station

1 A **station** is a place where trains and buses stop to let people on and off.
2 A **station** is also a building for the police or firefighters.

statue

A **statue** is something made of stone or metal that looks like a person or an animal.

steady *(steadier steadiest)*

If something is **steady**, it is not moving or shaking. *Mike held the ladder steady.*

steal *(steals stealing stole stolen)*

To **steal** means to take and keep something that does not belong to you. *The robbers stole millions of pounds worth of diamonds.*

steam

Steam is a cloud made of a lot of tiny drops that come from a liquid that is boiling. Some trains are powered by **steam**.

steep

A hill that is **steep** is hard to climb because it goes up quickly.

steel

Steel is a very hard strong metal that is used for making things such as tools, machines and cars.

stem

The **stem** of a plant is the long thin part that grows above the ground. Leaves and flowers grow on the **stem**.

step

1 You take a **step** every time you move your foot and put it in a different place.
2 A **step** is also one of the places where you put your foot when you go up or down stairs or a ladder. *The ladder has fifteen steps.*

stick

1 A **stick** is a long thin piece of wood.
2 *(sticks sticking stuck)* When you **stick** things together, you fix one thing to another using glue or tape. *Tara stuck a stamp on the envelope and posted her letter.*
3 *(sticks sticking stuck)* To **stick** also means to push something pointed into something else. *When Henry stuck a pin into the balloon it burst.*

still

1 If you are **still**, you do not move at all. *Please stand still.*
2 If something is **still** happening, it has not stopped. *I am still doing my homework.*

sting *(stings stinging stung)*

If an insect or a plant **stings** you, a sharp point goes into your skin and hurts you. *Ouch! That wasp just stung me!*

stir *(stirs stirring stirred)*

If you **stir** something, you move it around with something such as a spoon or a stick. *We helped Dad stir the cake mixture.*

stole, stolen Look at **steal**.

The dog stole my tennis ball. Somebody has stolen Laura's bike.

stomach

Your **stomach** is the part inside your body where food goes when you eat it.

stone

1 A **stone** is a small piece of rock.
2 A **stone** is also the hard seed in the middle of fruits such as cherries and peaches.

stood Look at **stand**.

She stood in the queue to buy tickets for the show.

stool

A **stool** is a small seat with no back or arms.

stop *(stops stopping stopped)*

1 If you **stop** doing something, you do not do it any more. *Maggie stopped reading and turned out the light.*
2 If something that was moving **stops**, it stands still. *The bus stops here. She stopped the car.*

store *(stores storing stored)*
If you **store** something, you put it somewhere so that you can use it later. *Squirrels collect nuts in autumn and store them for winter.*

storm
A **storm** is very bad weather with strong winds and a lot of rain or snow. Some **storms** also have thunder and lightning.

story *(stories)*
Some **stories** tell you about real things that have happened and others are made up. *Do you like ghost stories?*

straight
Something that is **straight** does not bend. *You should use a ruler to draw a straight line.*

strange
1 Something that is **strange** is different and surprising. *She was wearing very strange clothes.*
2 A **strange** place is somewhere you have not been before. *He was alone in a strange town.*

straw
1 **Straw** is the dry stems of plants such as wheat. *The pony sleeps on a bed of straw.*
2 A **straw** is a long tube made of paper or plastic for drinking through.

stream
A **stream** is a small river.

street
A **street** is a road in a town with buildings along both sides.

strength
Strength is how strong something is. *the strength of a lion.*

stretch *(stretches stretching stretched)*
If you **stretch** something, you pull it to make it longer or wider.

strict
If somebody is **strict**, they make sure everybody does what they say. *Our teacher is quite strict.*

string
1 **String** is thin rope. *We tied up the parcel with string.*
2 Some musical instruments such as guitars and violins have **strings** that you touch to play different notes.

strip
A **strip** is a long narrow piece of something. *Tear the paper into strips.*

stripe
A **stripe** is a line of colour on something. *Zebras have black and white stripes on their bodies.*

strong
1 If somebody is **strong**, they have a lot of power and can carry heavy things.
2 If something is **strong**, it is not easy to break.
3 If something has a **strong** taste or smell, you notice it easily. *Onions have a strong smell.*

stuck Look at **stick**.
I stuck a pin in the balloon and it burst with a bang.

stung Look at **sting**.
Jamie was stung by a bee.

submarine
A **submarine** is a special kind of boat that can travel deep under the sea.

suck *(sucks sucking sucked)*
If you **suck** something such as a sweet, you move it around and around in your mouth.

sudden
Something that is **sudden** happens quickly when you are not expecting it. *There was a sudden flash of lightning.*

sugar
Sugar is what you put in food or drinks to make them taste sweet.

suit
A **suit** is a jacket and a pair of trousers, or a jacket and a skirt, made from the same cloth.

suitcase
A **suitcase** is a kind of box with a handle that you carry your clothes in when you travel.

sum
When you do a **sum**, you work something out with numbers.

summer
Summer is the part of the year between spring and autumn. **Summer** is the hottest time of the year.

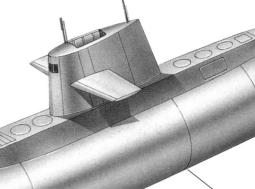
submarine

sun

The **Sun** is the bright star that shines and gives us heat and light during the day.

sunflower

A **sunflower** is a plant that can grow to be very tall. It has a very large flower with yellow petals.

sung Look at **sing**.

Have you sung this song before?

sunk Look at **sink**.

The boat has sunk to the bottom of the lake.

sunrise

Sunrise is the time in the early morning when the Sun comes up.

sunset

Sunset is the time in the evening when the Sun goes down. *We took a photo of the beautiful sunset.*

supermarket

A **supermarket** is a big shop that sells food and other things that people use in their homes.

supper

Supper is a meal that people eat in the evening. *I wonder what we're having for supper tonight?*

sure

If you are **sure** about something, you know that it is right or true. *Are you quite sure you closed the window?*

surface

The **surface** is the outside part of something. *The surface of the road is wet and slippery.*

surprise

A **surprise** is something that you did not expect to happen. *Don't tell Will about the party - it's going to be a surprise.*

swallow *(swallows swallowing swallowed)*

When you **swallow** food or drink, you let it go down your throat into your stomach.

swam Look at **swim**.

Kathy swam across the pool.

swan

A **swan** is a large white bird with a long neck. **Swans** live on water.

sweater

A **sweater** is something that you wear to keep you warm. It covers your arms and the top part of your body. **Sweaters** are often made of wool.

sweep *(sweeps sweeping swept)*

When you **sweep** a floor, you use a broom to clean it. *Dan swept up the leaves from the path.*

sweet

1 **Sweet** food and drink has the taste of sugar.

2 A **sweet** is a small piece of very **sweet** food.

swim *(swims swimming swam swum)*

When you **swim**, you move through water using your arms and legs.

swing

1 *(swings swinging swung)* When something **swings**, it moves from side to side or backwards and forwards through the air. *The monkey swung from a branch.*

2 A **swing** is a seat hanging from two ropes or chains that you sit on and move backwards and forwards through the air.

switch *(switches)*

A **switch** is something that you press or turn to start or stop something working. *If you press that switch all the lights will go out and we'll be in the dark!*

sword

A **sword** is a kind of long pointed knife that people in the past used for fighting.

swum Look at **swim**.

How many lengths of the pool have you swum today?

syrup

Syrup is a sweet sticky liquid made from sugar, water and sometimes fruit juices.

Tt

table

A **table** is a piece of furniture with legs and a flat top for putting things on.

table tennis

Table tennis is a game in which players use bats to hit a small ball over a net across a large table.

tadpole

A **tadpole** is a tiny creature with a long tail that lives in water. **Tadpoles** turn into frogs and toads. They have round black heads.

eggs

tadpole

tail

A **tail** is the part of an animal's body that grows out of the back. The back of an aeroplane is also called a **tail**.

tale

A **tale** is a story. *I have a book of fairy tales.*

talk *(talks talking talked)*

When you **talk**, you say words.

tall

A **tall** person or thing goes up a long way from the ground. *What is the tallest building in the world?*

tambourine

A **tambourine** is a musical instument a bit like a drum. You can hit or shake it to make the small metal pieces around its sides ring and play a tune.

tame

A **tame** animal is not wild so it is not dangerous or afraid of people. Pets are **tame** animals. Lions and tigers are not usually **tame**.

tap

A **tap** is something that you turn to make water flow out. Sinks and baths have **taps**.

tape

1 **Tape** is a strip of plastic with sticky stuff on one side that you use for sticking pieces of paper together.
2 A **tape** is also a strip of plastic in a plastic case that records sounds or pictures.

taste

1 A **taste** is what food or drink is like when it is in your mouth. *Honey has a sweet taste.*
2 *(tastes tasting tasted)* When you **taste** food or drink, you put a little of it in your mouth to see what it is like. *Can you taste this soup for me to see if there is enough salt in it?*

frog

taxi

A **taxi** is a car that you have to pay to travel in. You ask the driver to take you where you want to go. *We took a taxi to the station.*

tea

Tea is a drink that you make by adding hot water to the dried leaves of tea plants. *Mum asked me to make her a cup of tea.*

teach *(teaches teaching taught)*

To **teach** means to help somebody to learn something or to show them how to do something. *My uncle taught me to ride a bike. I am teaching my sister how to swim.*

teacher

A **teacher** is a person who teaches something.

team

A **team** is a group of people who play a game together on the same side. There are eleven players in a hockey **team**.

tear

Tears are drops of liquid that come from your eyes when you cry. *Tears ran down his face.*

tear *(tears tearing tore torn)*

When you **tear** something such as paper or cloth, you pull it apart. *Tim has torn his shirt on a rusty old nail.*

tease *(teases teasing teased)*

If you **tease** somebody, you annoy them and make jokes about them.

teeth Look at **tooth**.

Sharks have very sharp teeth.

telephone

You use a **telephone** for talking to people who are far away.

telescope

You use a **telescope** for looking at things that are far away, such as stars. **Telescopes** make things look bigger and closer.

television

A **television** is a machine that shows moving pictures with sound. A **television** looks like a box with a glass screen at the front. It is often called a TV or telly for short.

tell *(tells telling told)*

If you **tell** somebody something, you say it to them. *Tell me that story again.*

temperature

The **temperature** of something is how hot or cold it is.

tennis

Tennis is a game for two or four people. The players hit a ball backwards and forwards to each other over a net with a thing called a racket.

tent

A **tent** is a place to sleep in that is made of cloth. **Tents** are held up by poles and ropes.

term

A **term** is the time between holidays when schools are open.

terrible

If something is **terrible**, it is very bad. *a terrible storm.*

test

A **test** is a way of finding out how much somebody knows about something, or how well they can do something. *My aunt has just passed her driving test.*

thank *(thanks thanking thanked)*

When you **thank** somebody you say that you are pleased with something nice they have done for you.

theatre

A **theatre** is a building where people go to see plays.

thermometer

A **thermometer** is an instrument that shows how hot something is.

thick

1 Something that is **thick** measures a lot from one side to the other. *There is a thick wall around the building.*
2 If a liquid is **thick**, it does not flow easily. Yoghurt is thick.

thief *(thieves)*

A **thief** is a person who steals things. *The thieves stole several bikes from the shop.*

thin *(thinner thinnest)*

1 If something is **thin**, it does not measure very much from one side to the other. *It's dangerous to skate on thin ice.*
2 A **thin** person or animal does not weigh much.

think *(thinks thinking thought)*

When you **think**, you have ideas in your mind to work out or to decide things. *I'm thinking about what to give Mum for her birthday.*

thirsty *(thirstier thirstiest)*

When you are **thirsty**, you need something to drink.

thistle

A **thistle** is a plant with prickly leaves and a purple flower.

thorn

A **thorn** is a sharp point that grows on the stems of some plants such as roses.

thread

Thread is a long thin piece of something such as cotton or wool. *I need a needle and thread to sew on this button.*

throat

Your **throat** is the part at the back of your mouth, where food and air go down into your body.

throw *(throws throwing threw thrown)*

If you **throw** something, you make it leave your hand and fly through the air. *Robert threw a stick for his dog to fetch.*

thumb

Your **thumb** is the short thick finger at the side of your hand.

thunder

Thunder is a loud noise from the sky that comes after a flash of lightning when there is a storm.

ticket

A **ticket** is a small piece of paper that shows that you have paid for something. *We bought tickets to go and see the film.*

tickle *(tickles tickling tickled)*

If you **tickle** somebody, you keep touching their skin very gently to make them laugh.

tie

1 *(ties tying tied)* When you **tie** something such as string, you make a knot or bow in it.
2 A **tie** is a long strip of cloth that you tie around the collar of a shirt so it hangs down the front.

tiger

A **tiger** is a large wild animal of the cat family that lives in Asia. **Tigers** have orange-coloured fur with black stripes.

tight

1 If clothes are **tight**, they fit very closely to your body. *These shoes are so tight they hurt.*
2 If something is **tight**, it is done up so that it will not move easily. *Put the lid on tight so the paint doesn't spill.*

tile

A **tile** is a flat piece of hard material that is used to cover floors and walls. *The bathroom is covered in green and white tiles.*

time

Time is what we measure in seconds, minutes, hours, days, weeks, months and years. **Time** tells us when something happens or how long it happens for.

tin

1 Tin is a metal that is silver in colour. *a tin box.*
2 A **tin** is a metal container for food. *a tin of beans.*

tiny *(tinier tiniest)*

Something that is **tiny** is very very small. Sand is made up of **tiny** pieces of rock.

tip

1 The **tip** of something long and thin is the end of it. *Touch it with the tip of your finger.*
2 A **tip** is also a place where you can take rubbish.

tiptoe *(tiptoes tiptoeing tiptoed)*

If you **tiptoe**, you walk on your toes very quietly. *She tiptoed out of the baby's room.*

tired

When you are **tired**, you feel that you need to rest or to sleep.

tissue

A **tissue** is a piece of thin soft paper for blowing your nose on.

toad

A **toad** is an animal that looks like a big frog. **Toads** live mostly on land but they lay their eggs in water. They have rough dry skin.

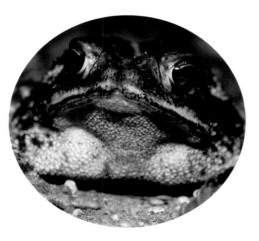

toast

Toast is a slice of bread that has been cooked on both sides so that it is brown.

toboggan

A **toboggan** is a kind of small sledge. It has a seat fixed to two long pieces of wood or metal that slide easily over snow.

toe

Your **toes** are the parts that you can move at the end of your feet. You have five **toes** on each foot.

told Look at **tell**.

Gran told us stories about when she was a little girl.

tomato *(tomatoes)*

A **tomato** is a soft round red fruit that we eat in salads.

tongue

Your **tongue** is the long pink part that moves around inside your mouth. Your **tongue** helps you to taste food and to talk.

tool

A **tool** is something that helps us to do work. *A saw is a tool for cutting wood.*

tooth *(teeth)*

1 A **tooth** is one of the hard white parts inside your mouth. We use our **teeth** to bite and chew food into pieces.
2 Teeth are also the sharp points on a comb or a saw.

toothbrush

A **toothbrush** is a small brush with a long handle for cleaning your teeth.

top

1 The **top** of something is the highest part of it. *We tied a big bow on the top of the box.*
2 A **top** is also the part that covers something such as a bottle or jar. *Don't forget to put the top back on your pen.*

torch *(torches)*

A **torch** is a small lamp that you can carry around to give light where you need it. **Torches** need batteries to make them work.

tore, torn Look at tear.

I tore the paper into tiny pieces. She has torn her jeans.

tornado *(tornadoes)*

A **tornado** is a storm with very strong winds that travel in circles and do a lot of damage to buildings and trees.

tortoise

A **tortoise** is an animal with a shell on its back. **Tortoises** move very slowly. **Tortoises** are reptiles.

total

A **total** is an amount that you get when you add two numbers together.

touch *(touches touching touched)*

1 If you **touch** something, you put your hand on it. *Millie tried to guess who it was by touching his face.*

2 If things are **touching**, there is no space between them. *We stood so close together that our shoulders were touching.*

tourist

A **tourist** is a person who is on holiday travelling and visiting interesting places. *Our town is busy in the summer because there are so many tourists.*

towel

A **towel** is a large piece of cloth that you use to dry yourself with.

tower

A **tower** is a tall thin building, or a tall thin part of a building.

town

A **town** is a place with streets, shops, houses and other buildings where people live and work.

toy

Toys are things you can play with. Dolls and kites are kinds of **toys**.

tractor

A **tractor** is a big strong vehicle that farmers use for pulling things.

traffic

Traffic is all the cars, buses, lorries and motorbikes moving along the road. *It took ages to get home because there was a lot of traffic.*

train

1 A **train** is a long vehicle that carries a lot of people from one place to another. **Trains** are pulled by engines and they run along railway lines.
2 *(trains training trained)* If you **train** a person or an animal to do something, you teach them how to do it. *We have trained our dog to sit when we tell her to.*

train

trap

A **trap** is something that is used to catch animals. *a mouse trap.*

travel *(travels travelling travelled)*

When you **travel**, you go from one place to another. *We travelled to Spain by boat and car.*

tray

A **tray** is a flat piece of wood or metal that you use for carrying food and drink on.

tread *(treads treading trod trodden)*

When you **tread** on something, you put your foot down on it.

treasure

Treasure is a big pile of gold, silver, jewels and other valuable things. *This map shows where the pirate's treasure is buried.*

tree

A **tree** is a big plant with branches and leaves growing from a thick stem called a trunk that is made of wood.

trick

1 A **trick** is something clever and amazing that you can do. *The magician's best trick was when he made a bird come out of his hat.*

2 A **trick** is also a thing that somebody does to make you believe something that is not true. *My brother played a trick on me - he put a toy spider in my drink.*

trip

1 A **trip** is a short journey. *Yesterday we went on a school trip to London.*

2 (trips tripping tripped) If you **trip**, you knock your foot against something and you fall over. *I tripped on the step.*

trod, trodden Look at tread.

I trod on a snail. You should not have trodden on the grass.

trousers

Trousers are something that you wear. **Trousers** cover the lower part of your body and each leg.

truck

A **truck** is a lorry. People use **trucks** to carry heavy things from place to place by road.

true

1 If something is **true**, it is right. *Is it true that ice is frozen water?*

2 If something is **true**, it really happened. *That's a true story.*

trumpet

A **trumpet** is a musical instrument made of metal. You blow into it to make sounds.

trunk

1 A **trunk** is the thick stem of a tree. A **trunk** is made of wood.

2 A **trunk** is also an elephant's long nose. The elephant uses its **trunk** to lift things and to carry food and water to its mouth.

3 A **trunk** is also a large box for keeping things in or for carrying things on a long journey.

trust (trusts trusting trusted)

If you **trust** somebody, you believe that they will do what they promise and will not do anything to hurt you. *Can I trust you to behave yourself while I'm out?*

truth

When you tell the **truth**, you are saying what is true. *You didn't break the glass? Is that the truth?*

tube

1 A **tube** is something that is long, thin and hollow such as a metal or plastic pipe.

2 A **tube** is also a long container for holding soft stuff such as toothpaste.

tunnel

A **tunnel** is a long hole under the ground or through a hill. *We saw the steam train come through the tunnel.*

turn

1 (turns turning turned) When something **turns**, it moves round. When a car moves, its wheels **turn**. *Jane turned her trousers inside out to sew them up.*

2 (turns turning turned) When something **turns** into something else, it changes. Water **turns** into steam when you boil it. *The farmer turned the milk into cheese.*

3 If it is your **turn** to do something, it is time for you to do it. *It's Maria's turn to take the dog for a walk today.*

twig

A **twig** is a very small branch of a tree or bush. *Collect some twigs so we can light a fire.*

twin

Twins are two children who have the same mother and who were born at the same time.

twist (twists twisting twisted)

When you **twist** two pieces of thread or wire together, you wrap them around each other many times. *She twisted the strings together.*

tyre

A **tyre** is the rubber cover around the outside of a wheel filled with air. *My bike has a flat tyre.*

Uu

ugly *(uglier ugliest)*
If something is **ugly**, it is not nice to look at.

umbrella
You hold an **umbrella** over your head to keep you dry when it rains. It has a piece of cloth stretched over wires and joined to a long handle.

uncle
Your **uncle** is your father's brother, your mother's brother or the husband of your aunt.

underneath
If something is **underneath** something else, it is below it. *The cat was asleep underneath the blanket.*

underground
Underground means below the ground. *Rabbits live underground in holes called burrows.*

understand *(understands understanding understood)*
If you **understand** something, you know what it means or how it works. *I couldn't understand what she said because she didn't speak very good English.*

undress *(undresses undressing undressed)*
When you **undress**, you take off your clothes.

unhappy
If you are **unhappy**, you are sad.

uniform
A **uniform** is a set of special clothes that show that people belong to a group. Nurses and soldiers wear **uniforms**.

universe
The **universe** is the Earth, the Sun, the Moon, the stars and everything in space.

university
A **university** is a place where people can go to study after they have left school.

untidy
If things are **untidy**, they are not in the right place. *Your room is very untidy - there are books and clothes all over the floor.*

unusual
If something is **unusual**, it is not ordinary or what we usually expect. *It is unusual for it to rain in the desert.*

upset
If you are **upset**, you feel unhappy. *Natasha was upset when her friend forgot her birthday.*

upside down
If something is **upside down**, the bottom is at the top and the top is at the bottom. *Bats always hang upside down.*

upstairs
Upstairs means in a higher part of a building. *There are four bedrooms upstairs.*

urgent
If something is **urgent**, it must be done straight away. *Please call an ambulance. It's urgent.*

useful
Something that is **useful** helps you to do something. *Keep that box - it will be useful for putting your toys in.*

usual
If something is **usual**, it happens most of the time. *We went to the swimming pool on Saturday as usual.*

usually
Usually means nearly always. *I usually watch television for a little while after school.*

Vv

vacuum cleaner
A **vacuum cleaner** is an electric machine that picks up dust and dirt from carpets.

valley
A **valley** is the low land between hills or mountains.

valuable
If something is **valuable**, it is worth a lot of money. *This gold watch is very valuable.*

van
A **van** is a small covered lorry for carrying things by road.

vegetable
A **vegetable** is a part of a plant that you can eat. Cabbages, potatoes, carrots, peas and beans are **vegetables**.

vehicle
A **vehicle** is a machine for carrying things or people from one place to another on land. Buses, cars, lorries and bicycles are all **vehicles**.

vet
A **vet** is a kind of doctor who looks after animals that are ill or hurt. *Ian wants to be a vet and look after wild animals in Africa.*

video
1 A **video** is a tape that records pictures and sounds so that you can play them on a television set.
2 A **video** is also a machine for recording and playing pictures and sounds.

view
A **view** is everything that you can see from one place. *You get a good view of the town from the bridge.*

village
A **village** is a small group of houses and other buildings in the country.

vine
A **vine** is a climbing plant that grapes grow on.

vinegar
Vinegar is a liquid with a sour taste that you put on food such as chips.

violent
A **violent** person is very strong and very rough.

violet
A **violet** is a small plant with purple or white flowers.

violin
A **violin** is a musical instrument made of wood. It has four strings. You play a **violin** by moving a long stick called a bow backwards and forwards across the strings.

visit *(visits visiting visited)*
When you **visit** somebody, you go to see them. *We visit our granddad every Saturday.*

voice
Your **voice** is the sound that you make when you talk or sing.

volcano *(volcanoes)*
A **volcano** is a mountain with a hole called a crater in the top. Sometimes hot liquid rock and gases shoot out of the crater. *The village was destroyed by the liquid rock from the volcano.*

vote *(votes voting voted)*
If you **vote** for somebody or something, you choose them by putting a mark on a piece of paper next to their name, or by putting up your hand.

voyage
A **voyage** is a long journey. *They went on a voyage into space.*

vulture
A **vulture** is a large bird that lives in hot countries and feeds on dead animals.

Ww

wait (waits waiting waited)
When you **wait**, you stay in one place because you are expecting something to happen. *Wait here until I get back.*

wake (wakes waking woke woken)
When you **wake** up, you stop sleeping. *What time do you usually wake up in the morning?*

walk (walks walking walked)
When you **walk**, you move along by putting one of your feet in front of the other.

wall
1 A **wall** is one of the sides of a room or building.
2 A **wall** is also something made of stone or brick that is put around a field or garden.

wallet
A **wallet** is a flat container for paper money that you can carry in a pocket or a handbag. *Always keep your wallet safe.*

walrus
(walruses)
A **walrus** is a large sea mammal with long curved tusks and whiskers.

wand
A **wand** is a kind of short stick that fairies and magicians use to help them do magic.

want (wants wanting wanted)
When you **want** something, you would like to have it. *Do you want anything to eat?*

war
A **war** is when the armies of different countries are fighting one another.

ward
A **ward** is a large room in a hospital with beds in it.

wardrobe
A **wardrobe** is a place for keeping clothes in.

warm
Warm means a little hot but not too hot. *This sweater will keep you warm in cold weather.*

warn (warns warning warned)
If you **warn** somebody, you tell them that something bad or dangerous is going to happen. *He warned us not to go out in the boat because there was going to be a storm.*

wash (washes washing washed)
When you **wash** something, you make it clean with soap and water. *We washed our feet.*

wasp
A **wasp** is a flying insect with black and yellow stripes. **Wasps** can sting.

waste (wastes wasting wasted)
If you **waste** something, you use more of it than you need to. *Don't waste all those sheets of paper - you can draw on the other side.*

watch
1 (watches watching watched) If you **watch** something, you look at it for a time. *We watched a film on television.*
2 (watches) A **watch** is a small clock that you wear on your wrist.

water
1 **Water** is a clear liquid. It fills lakes, rivers and seas. It falls from the sky as rain. All living things need **water** to live.
2 (waters watering watered) If you **water** plants you pour **water** onto them.

waterfall
A **waterfall** is a place on a river where the water falls down over high rocks.

wave
1 A **wave** is a moving curved line on a sea or lake.
2 (waves waving waved) If you **wave**, you move your hand up and down or from side to side. *Zoe waved goodbye to her friends.*

wax
Wax is something that is used to make candles and polish. **Wax** melts when it gets warm.

weak

Somebody or something that is **weak** does not have much strength. *The pony was so weak that it could not stand up.*

wear *(wears wearing wore worn)*

1 When you **wear** clothes, you have them on your body. *Have you worn that hat before?*
2 When something **wears** out, it becomes weak and it cannot be used any more, because you have used it so much. *He wore out six pairs of boots when he walked from London to Scotland.*

weather

The **weather** is what it is like outside. For example, if it's rainy, sunny or snowing.

web

A **web** is a thin net of threads that a spider makes to catch insects to eat.

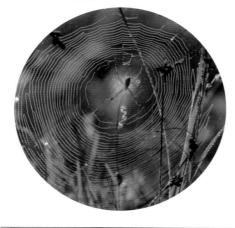

wedding

A **wedding** is a special time when a man and woman get married to each other.

week

A **week** is an amount of time. There are seven days in a **week.**

weigh *(weighs weighing weighed)*

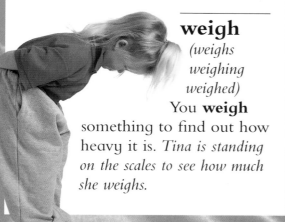

You **weigh** something to find out how heavy it is. *Tina is standing on the scales to see how much she weighs.*

weight

The **weight** of something is how heavy it is. *Can you guess the weight of the parcel?*

well

1 *(better best)* If you are **well**, you feel good and healthy. *I don't feel well.*
2 *(better best)* If you do something **well**, you are good at it. *John plays the trumpet very well.*
3 A **well** is a deep hole that people dig in the ground to get water or oil.

west

West is the direction where the Sun goes down in the evening. **West** is the opposite of east.

wet *(wetter wettest)*

If something is **wet**, it is covered in water or full of water. *My doll got wet when it fell in the pond.*

whale

A **whale** is a very big animal that lives in the sea. **Whales** are mammals but they look more like big fish.

wheat

Wheat is a plant that farmers grow. Its seeds are used to make flour for bread.

wheel

A **whee**l is a round thing that turns. Bikes and roller-skates have **wheels** to help them move along the ground.

wheelchair

A **wheelchair** is a chair with wheels. People use **wheelchairs** when they cannot walk very well.

whisker

Whiskers are the long hairs that animals such as dogs and cats have on their faces.

whisper *(whispers whispering whispered)*

When you **whisper**, you speak in a very quiet voice. *Julie whispered something in my ear.*

whistle

1 *(whistles whistling whistled)* When you **whistle**, you blow through your lips to make a high musical sound. *The dog came back when Mia whistled.*
2 A **whistle** is a small instrument that you blow through to make a high sound.

whole

The **whole** of something is all of it. *We spent the whole morning at the pool and didn't go home until after lunch-time.*

wide

Something that is **wide** measures a lot from one side to the other. *Motorways are much wider than ordinary roads.*

wife

A man's **wife** is the woman that he is married to.

wild

Animals that are **wild** do not live with people. They find their own food. Foxes and deer are **wild** animals. **Wild** plants are not grown by people. *The field was full of beautiful wild flowers.*

win *(wins winning won)*

When you **win**, you do better than everybody else in a game or race.

wind

Wind is air that is moving fast. *The wind blew the leaves everywhere.*

windmill

A **windmill** is a tall building with sails on the front that the wind turns as it blows. As the sails move, they work machines that can turn wheat into flour or that can make electricity.

window

A **window** is a hole in a wall filled with glass. **Windows** let in light from outside.

wing

Wings are the parts that animals such as birds and insects use for flying. Aeroplanes also have **wings** to help them to stay up in the air.

winter

Winter is the part of the year between autumn and spring. **Winter** is usually the coldest time of the year.

wipe *(wipes wiping wiped)*

If you **wipe** something, you clean or dry it by rubbing it with a cloth. *Please wipe up after you.*

wire

Wire is a long thin piece of metal that is easy to bend. **Wire** is used to make fences. Electricity moves along **wires**.

wish

1 *(wishes wishing wished)*
If you **wish** for something, you want it to happen very much. *I wish I had skates like yours.*
2 A **wish** is something you would like very much to happen. *Close your eyes and make a wish.*

witch *(witches)*

A **witch** is a woman in fairy stories who can do magic things.

wives Look at **wife**.

King Henry the Eighth had six wives.

wizard

A **wizard** is a man in fairy stories who can do magic things.

woke, woken Look at **wake**.

I woke up in the middle of the night. You must have woken the baby up when you came in.

wolf *(wolves)*

A **wolf** is a wild animal that looks like a dog.

woman *(women)*

A **woman** is a grown-up female. Girls grow up to be **women**.

won Look at **win**.
Michael won the race.

wonderful
Something that is **wonderful** is very good or amazing. *We had a wonderful holiday.*

wood
1 Wood is what trees are made of. We use **wood** to make furniture like tables and chairs.
2 A **wood** is a lot of trees growing together. *We went for a walk in the woods.*

wool
Wool is the soft thick hair that grows on sheep. We spin **wool** and use it to make things such as jumpers and scarves. *a ball of wool.*

word
We use **words** when we speak or write. Each **word** is a sound or a group of letters of the alphabet that means something. *"Dog" and "today" are words.*

wore Look at **wear**.
Joe wore a yellow jacket.

work
1 Work is what somebody does to earn money, or something that they have to do. *Do you enjoy going to work everyday?*

2 *(works working worked)* When you **work**, you do or make something, often as a job. *Hilary works in a car factory.*
3 *(works working worked)* If a machine **works**, it goes as it should do. *Do you know how to make this video work?*

world
The **world** is the planet that we live on.

worm
A **worm** is a small long thin creature with no legs. **Worms** live in the ground.

worn Look at **wear**.
This is the first time this year that I have worn this shirt.

worry *(worries worrying worried)*
When you **worry**, you cannot stop thinking about problems or things that may happen. *Dad always worries when I get home late.*

worth
The amount something is worth is how much you must pay to have it. *This painting is worth a lot of money.*

wrap *(wraps wrapping wrapped)*
When you **wrap** something, you cover it with something else such as paper or cloth. *Rachel is wrapping a present.*

wrinkle
A **wrinkle** is a line on somebody's face. *My gran's face is full of wrinkles.*

wrist
Your **wrist** is the part of your arm where it joins your hand. *You can wear a watch on your wrist for telling the time.*

write *(writes writing wrote written)*
When you **write**, you put words on paper so that people can read them. *Mel is writing a letter to her cousin in Australia.*

wrong
Something that is **wrong** is not right. *I think that it is always wrong to tell lies.*

Xx

X-ray

An **X-ray** is a special kind of photograph that shows the inside of your body. *The doctor took an X-ray of his head to see if he had broken any bones.*

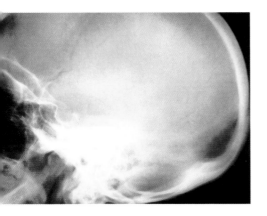

xylophone

A **xylophone** is a musical instrument with flat wooden or metal bars that you hit with small hammers to make music.

Yy

yacht

A **yacht** is a large boat with sails or an engine. Some **yachts** are very fast and are used for racing.

yawn *(yawns yawning yawned)*

When you **yawn**, you open your mouth wide and breathe in. People usually **yawn** when they are tired.

year

A **year** is an amount of time. There are twelve months in a **year**. *Hassan will be seven years old on his next birthday.*

yell *(yells yelling yelled)*

If you **yell**, you shout something very loudly. *"Come here!" she yelled across the street.*

yoghurt

Yoghurt is a food made from milk. You sometimes eat **yoghurt** mixed with fruit. *My favourite yoghurt is raspberry.*

yolk

A yolk is the yellow part in the middle of an egg. *Ben likes a soft yolk in his egg.*

young

A person or animal that is **young** was born not very long ago. **Young** people are children. **Young** dogs are called puppies, and **young** cats are called kittens. *What is a young sheep called?*

Zz

zebra

A **zebra** is an animal that looks like a horse with black and white stripes. **Zebras** live in Africa.

zero

Zero is the number 0.

zigzag

A **zigzag** is a line that bends sharply one way and then the other.

zip

A **zip** is made of two long pieces of metal or plastic with parts that fit together to hold two edges of cloth together. Some trousers and bags have **zips**.

zoo

A **zoo** is a place where a lot of different wild animals are kept so that people can go there to look at them.

Useful facts

Days of the week
Sunday
Monday
Tuesday
Wednesday
Thursday
Friday
Saturday

Months of the year
January
February
March
April
May
June
July
August
September
October
November
December

This calendar shows us the days of the week.

A rainbow has many colours.

Colours
Maroon
Red
Blue
Turquoise

Yellow
Green
Purple
Violet

Lilac
Orange
Brown
Black

White
Cream
Grey
Pink

Flat shapes
square
rectangle
circle
oval
star
triangle
diamond
heart
semi-circle
pentagon (five sides)
hexagon (six sides)
octagon (eight sides)

square

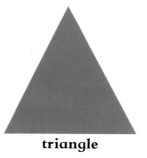

triangle

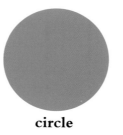

circle

rectangle

Numbers

1	one	first
2	two	second
3	three	third
4	four	fourth
5	five	fifth
6	six	sixth
7	seven	seventh
8	eight	eighth
9	nine	ninth
10	ten	tenth
11	eleven	eleventh
12	twelve	twelfth
13	thirteen	thirteenth
14	fourteen	fourteenth
15	fifteen	fifteenth
16	sixteen	sixteenth
17	seventeen	seventeenth
18	eighteen	eighteen
19	nineteen	nineteenth
20	twenty	twentieth
21	twenty-one	twenty-first
22	twenty-two	twenty-second
23	twenty-three	twenty-third
30	thirty	thirtieth
40	forty	fortieth
50	fifty	fiftieth
60	sixty	sixtieth
70	seventy	seventieth
80	eighty	eightieth
90	ninety	nintieth
100	a hundred	hundredth
101	a hundred and one	
	one hundred and first	
1,000	a thousand	thousandth
1,000,000	a million	a millionth

Words we use all the time

Check your spelling of these common words.

about
all
also
although
am
among
an
and
another
any
anybody
anyhow
anything
anywhere
are
aren't (are not)
as
at
away
be
became
because
been
before
being
below
beside
between
beyond
both
came
can
can't (can not)
come
comes
coming
could
couldn't (could not)
did
didn't (did not)
do
does
doesn't (does not)
doing
done
don't (do not)
each
either
every
everybody
everyone
everywhere
far
from

gallon
gave
get
getting
give
given
go
goes
going
gone
got
had
hadn't (had not)
happen
has
hasn't (has not)
have
haven't (have not)
having
he
hello
her
here
hers
he's (he is)
his
him
I'd (I had or I would)
if
I'm (I am)
in
indoors
inside
into
is
isn't (is not)
it
its
it's (it is)
I've (I have)
just
kilogram
kilometre
least
less
let's (let us)
litre
lot
lovable
made
make
many
march
may

me
metre
might
mine
more
most
much
my
myself
neither
no
nobody
none
no one
nothing
nowhere
now
of
off
on
once
or
other
our
ours
out
over
perfect
perhaps
player
popular
pound
put
putting
really
red (colour)
same
self
shall
she
should
shouldn't (should not)
so
some
somebody
someone
something
sometimes
somewhere
such
take
taken
taking
tell

than
thank
that
the
their
theirs
them
then
there
these
they
they're
this
those
though
thought
through
to
today
told
tomorrow
tonight
too
took
try
unless
until
up
us
use
very
was
wasn't (was not)
we
welcome
well
we'll (we shall)
went
were
weren't (were not)
what
when
where
which
who
whose
why
won't (will not)
would
would not (wouldn't)
yet
you
you're (you are)
you've (you have)

Acknowledgements

The publishers would like to thank the following artists who have
contributed to this book:

Mike Atkinson; Julie Banyard; Andy Beckett; Martin Camm; Kuo
Kang Chen; Wayne Ford; John James; Aziz Khan; Alan Male
(Linden Artists); Mel Pickering (Contour Publishing); Terry Riley;
Peter Sarson; Mike Saunders; Guy Smith (Mainline Design);
Roger Smith; Roger Stewart; Michael White(Temple Rogers).

All commissioned photography by **Patrick Spillane (Creative Vision)**.
All other photographs supplied by **Miles Kelly Archives**.

The publishers would also like to thank the following children for
appearing in photographs throughout this book:

Bemi Akinwumi; Fola Akinwumi; Alex Bermingham; Sophie
DeHavilland; Michael Forsyth; Ruwa Foster; Afrika Green;
William Hawthorn; James Haygreen; Abbey Herrington; Jacob
Lawrence; Sual Leslie; Jacob McGill; Sam McGill; Pispa
Mackenzie; Emma Nakazato; Ryan Oyeyemi; Julia Robinson;
Dulcie Rutter; Jacob Rutter; Eriko Sato; Luke Rutter; Shirine
Sayfoo; Julia Smerdon; Katie Smerdon; Helen Thurlow; Joe
Werker; Thomas Wopshot.